영국 아재 데이브의

매일 영어 교습소

Dave's Daily English

영국 아재 데이브의
매일 영어 교습소

글쓴이·그린이 데이브 피콕 David Peacock
펴낸이 정규도
펴낸곳 (주)다락원
초판 1쇄 발행 2021년 7월 20일
초판 2쇄 발행 2023년 6월 30일

책임편집 장의연
본문 디자인 하태호
표지 디자인 이보나
전산편집 조수영

다락원 경기도 파주시 문발로 211
내용문의: (02)736-2031 내선 523
구입문의: (02)736-2031 내선 250~252
Fax: (02)732-2037
출판등록 1977년 9월 16일 제406-2008-000007호

ISBN 978-89-277-0140-8 13740

www.darakwon.co.kr
다락원 홈페이지를 방문하시면 상세한 출판정보와 함께 동영상
강좌, MP3자료 등 다양한 어학 정보를 얻으실 수 있습니다

영국 아재 데이브의

매일 영어 교습소

Dave's Daily English

Another
feather
in
your
cap

데이브 선생이 직접 그리고 씀

 DARAKWON

Welcome to
Dave's Daily English!

데이브의 매일 영어 교습소에 오신 걸 환영합니다

English can be fun, but some expressions can, at first, be confusing. For example—'My mind boggles!'. Do you have any idea what this expression means or how to use it? '영국 아재 데이브의 매일 영어 교습소' is full of useful, interesting and fun English expressions that can be found in everyday conversation in English speaking countries all over the world.

영어는 재미있기도 하지만 어떤 표현은 처음 들으면 무슨 말인지 도무지 알 수 없을 때도 있습니다. 예를 들어, My mind boggles! 이 표현이 무슨 뜻인지, 어떻게 사용하는지 아시나요? 『영국 아재 데이브의 매일 영어 교습소』에는 전 세계 영어권 국가에서 일상 대화에 쓰는 실용적이고 흥미로우면서 재미있는 영어 표현을 담았습니다.

In this book, 150 expressions are delivered to you in 2 ways:
• a monologue describing a realistic situation.
• a true to life, natural conversation between two people.

이 책에서는 150개의 표현을 두 가지 방법으로 설명합니다.
• 현실적인 상황을 설명하는 글
• 실제 삶에서 두 사람의 자연스러운 대화

Each expression is also accompanied by a colourful drawing to help you to remember the expression. Additionally, you can listen to audio recordings of native English speakers describing the situation and having conversations that you will find in this book.

모든 표현은 그림을 함께 그려 넣어 기억하기에 도움이 되도록 했습니다. 그리고 이 책의 모든 상황 설명과 대화 내용은 원어민이 녹음한 오디오로 들을 수 있습니다.

By the way, 'My mind boggles!' means something that is difficult to imagine or understand because it is so amazing, strange, or complicated. It's also in this book, so please look it up.

아무튼, My mind boggles!는 너무 놀랍고 이상하고 복잡해서, 상상하거나 이해하기 힘든 상황을 의미합니다. 이 책에도 실려 있으니 한번 찾아보세요.

Finally, I would like to thank my wonderful wife, Theresa Yi, my awesome coordinator, Jinsun Park and my good friend, Greg Dawson, for their help in making this book. I dedicate this book to my parents for my wonderful upbringing and to all of my students – past, present and future.

끝으로, 저는 이 책을 출판하도록 도움을 준 나의 멋진 아내 이데레사와 훌륭한 코디네이터 박진선, 그리고 저의 소중한 친구인 그렉 도슨에게 진심으로 고마움을 전하고 싶습니다. 무한한 사랑과 신뢰로 나를 키워주신 부모님과 과거 현재 미래의 나의 모든 학생들에게 이 책을 바칩니다.

David Peacock

Full of useful colloquial expressions!

네이티브 표현이 가득합니다

1 한방에 통하는 비법은 이디엄에 있다

인식하지 못하겠지만 여러분은 관용어를 꽤 많이 사용하고 있다. 오늘도 '등골 빠지게' 일하신 분 많을 것이다. 집에 와서 영어공부 한번 해보겠다고 책을 펴지만 '마음은 콩밭에 가' 있기 십상이다(속담). '작심삼일(성어)'이라도 삼 일마다 반복하면 꾸준한 거 아니냐고 억지부리기도 한다.

영어도 마찬가지다. 이디엄이니 속담이니 외국어에서 유래한 표현까지, 따로 알아둬야 뭔 소린지 알 수 있는 표현이 많다. 여기서는 익숙한 표현인 '이디엄'으로 통쳐서 소개했지만, 이 책에는 영어를 이해하고 표현할 때 꼭 알아야 할 이디엄(idiom), 속담(proverb)을 포함한 여러 구어 표현(colloquial expression)을 골라서 보여준다.

2 짧은 영어 읽기로 리딩 두려움을 없앤다

보아하니 표현 배우는 책 같은데 리딩이 웬 말인가 싶겠지만, 모든 표현은 쓰이는 상황을 알아야 그 상황이 왔을 때 알아채고 제대로 쓸 수 있다. 바로 그 상황을 알려주면서 리딩 감각도 익힐 수 있다는 게 이 책의 장

점이다. 겁 먹을 필요 없다. 상황 설명글은 단어와 문장 구조가 단순해서 생각보다 술술 읽힌다. 본인이 영어를 잘하는 것 같은 착각마저 들 것이다.

3 네이티브 표현 150개가 저절로 스며든다

억지로 외워봤자 바로 까먹는게 단어와 표현이다. 제발 외우지 마시고, 그냥 슬슬 읽으시길 권한다. 성에 안 차면 여러 번 읽자. 이왕이면 소리 내어 읽는 것을 권한다. 우연히 영화나 원서에서 읽었던 표현을 만나고 무슨 뜻인지 상황까지 떠오르는 벅찬 체험이 기다리고 있으니 걱정 말고 그냥 읽자.

4 반듯한 영국 영어의 매력에 흠뻑 빠져든다

영국 영어와 미국 영어는 일부 표현이 다를 뿐 근본적인 차이는 없다. 가장 큰 차이가 발음인데, 굴리고 흘려서 좌절감만 안겨주는 미국 발음보다 영국 발음이 듣기도 하기도 수월하다. 미국 사람들도 반한다는 교양 있는 영국 영어에 흠뻑 빠져 보자.

데이브 선생이 알려주는
이 책 공부법

:

Just read, and
feel the expressions!

일단 읽고 표현을 느끼세요

1 영문을 읽는다

일단, 왼쪽 페이지 먼저 읽어볼 것을 추천한다. 왼쪽 페이지는 영어로만 되어 있다. 원서 읽는 다고 생각하고 슬슬 읽어 보자.

2 표현을 추측한다

색으로 표시된 부분이 우리가 해결해야 할 구어 표현이다. 그림을 보고 글 내용까지 미루어 짐작해서 뜻을 추측해 보자. 아마 대략 감이 올 것이다.

3 대화를 읽는다

같은 표현이 대화 속에서 다시 나온다. 이제쯤 이면 이 표현이 어떤 뜻인지 좀 더 확실해졌을 것이다.

5 한국어 해석은 필요한 때만

한국어 해석은 참고만 하자. 일대일 대응식 번역은 영어 습득에 도움이 안 된다. 그래서 여기에도 딱딱한 직역은 지양하고 뜻 전달 위주로 번역했다.

4 의미를 확인한다

오른쪽 페이지 상단에는 이 표현의 정의가 영어로 적혀 있다. 가능하면 영문을 먼저 읽어 보고 한국어 해석을 참고하자. 당신도 할 수 있다.

6 정통 영국 발음으로 듣는다

큐알코드를 찍어 정통 영국 발음으로 들어보자. 신기하게도 꽤 잘 들린다. 한 번 읽었기 때문이기도 하고, 정석적이고 클리어한 영국 발음 때문이기도 하다. 듣기 좋은 건 자주 듣자.

Contents

영어하기
좋은
날!

Dave's Daily English

일러두기

하나. 미국 영어는 달리 쓰는 단어에는 따로 표시하고,
　　 미국에서 사용하는 형태를 따로 알려드립니다.
　　 예 favourite → favorite [AM]

둘. 오른쪽 페이지 작은 그림에는 그림 안에 들어 있는 영어 문장과
　　 표현을 직역해서 보여드립니다. 글자 그대로 옮겼기 때문에
　 어색할 수도 있습니다. 하지만 읽어 보시면 해당 구어 표현이 가진
　　 원래 의도를 이해할 수 있어, 쉽게 기억됩니다.

셋. 오른쪽 페이지 한국어 뜻과 표현 아래에 Com, For, Inf 표시는
　　 각각 Common(일상적), Formal(격식적), Informal(비격식적)을
　　 나타냅니다. 상황에 맞게 사용해보세요.

A barrel of laughs

I love watching live stand up comedy shows.
One of my favourite* comedians only tells 'one-liner'
jokes. He's **a barrel of laughs**!

Tyler: My friend, Tony, is really funny. He's always telling jokes and he's really good at mimicking* different accents.

Gail: Yeah! I met him at a party a few weeks ago. He's **a real barrel of laughs**!

엄청 웃긴 사람/것
a barrel of laughs
Com/Inf

Someone or something that is very
funny. It is often used in a sarcastic way.
엄청 웃긴 사람이나 상황. 종종 비꼬는 투로 쓴다.

쟤는
웃음통이야

He's a
barrel of laughs

전 생방송 스탠드 업 코미디 쇼 보는 것을 좋아해요. 제가
좋아하는 코미디언 한 명은 '짤막한 농담'으로 우스갯소리를
합니다. 그 사람은 **엄청나게 웃긴 사람**이에요!

*favorite [AM]

**이렇게
말하자:**

타일러: 내 친구 토니는 진짜 웃겨. 걔는 항상 농담을 하고, 다른 말투
흉내 내는 것을 정말 잘해.

게일: 맞아! 몇 주 전 파티에서 토니를 만났는데, **진짜 웃긴
사람**이더라.

*mimic 흉내 내다(분사 형태로 쓸 때는 mimicking, mimicked처럼 k를 넣어 쓰는 것에 주의)

a couch potato

A lot of people are very active in their free time. Some people enjoy doing sports or going out with friends, but me? I like being **a couch potato**. I like to just relax at home and watch movies.

IN A REAL CONVERSATION

Cindy: How was your weekend?

Dave: Excellent! I spent the whole weekend sitting on the sofa in my pajamas watching TV, eating, and drinking. I was **a** complete **couch potato**!

소파족, 게으름뱅이
a couch potato
Com/Inf

A person who spends a great deal of time sitting on the sofa doing nothing constructive and watching television
장시간 소파에 앉아 건설적인 것은 아무것도 하지 않고 TV만 보는 사람

소파 감자

많은 사람은 여유 시간이 있을 때 굉장히 활동적이죠. 어떤 사람들은 운동하거나 친구들과 어울리길 좋아하지만, 저요? 전 **집콕**(집에만 있는 것)을 좋아해요. 전 그냥 집에서 쉬면서 영화 보는 게 좋아요.

이렇게 말하자:

신디: 주말 어떻게 지냈어?

데이브: 최고였어! 난 주말 내내 잠옷 입고 소파에 앉아서, TV 보고 먹고 마시고 했지. 완전 **소파에 들러붙어** 있었어!

I love '**fly on the wall**' documentaries. I really enjoy watching* real people (not actors) being filmed* in real, everyday situations. Watching real people in real situations is much more exciting than watching actors acting.

IN A REAL CONVERSATION

Blake: I have a date tonight with the most beautiful girl I've ever met!

Hailey: Really? Good for you!

Blake: I'm SO nervous. I really want her to be my girlfriend. I'm worried I might say or do something wrong on the date.

Hailey: Haha, I'm sure you'll be okay, but I'd love to be **a fly on the wall** to see how it goes!

염탐꾼
a fly on the wall
Com/Inf

003. MP3

A person who secretly observes a
particular event when it happens
어떤 특정한 사건이 일어났을 때 몰래 관찰하는 사람

벽에 붙은 파리

전 **관찰** 다큐를 정말 좋아합니다. 전 일상에서 (배우가 아닌)
일반인을 실제 상황으로 촬영한 것을 보는 것을 정말 즐거요.
일반인을 일상 상황에서 촬영한 것을 보는 게 배우가 연기하는
걸 보는 것보다 훨씬 재미있어요.

* enjoy -ing – 하는 것을 즐기다
* watch+사람+동작 (사람)이 (동작)하는 것을 보다

**이렇게
말하자:**

블레이크: 오늘 저녁에 내가 지금까지 만났던 사람 중 가장 아름다운
여자와 데이트할 거야!

헤일리: 정말? 잘됐다!

블레이크: 나 너무 떨려. 난 정말 그분이 내 여자친구가 되면 좋겠어.
내가 데이트 때 뭘 잘못 말하거나 실수할까 봐 걱정돼.

헤일리: 하하, 괜찮을 거라고 확신하지만, 어떻게 되어 가는지
숨어서 보고 싶네!

A frog in my throat

This morning, I was acting in a video for my blog but in the middle of my long speech, I got **a frog in my throat** and couldn't speak clearly. So I had to start from the beginning again. I think I'm catching a cold.

Judy: Hey, Joe. How are you?

Joe: (Speaking hoarsely) Not bad, thanks.

Judy: Oh, but your voice sounds terrible! Are you sure you're okay?

Joe: Yes. I just ate some really spicy curry and it's given me **a frog in my throat**. I'll be okay in a few minutes.

목 잠김
a frog
in one's throat
Com/Inf

Having difficulty in speaking because your throat feels dry and you want to cough. When you have a throat problem, your voice sounds similar to a frog.

목이 마르고 기침을 하고 싶어서 말이 잘 안 나오는 것. 목에 문제가 생기면 개구리와 비슷한 소리가 난다.

내 목구멍에
개구리가 있어

오늘 아침, 제 블로그를 위해 동영상 촬영을 하고 있었는데, 길게 말하는 중간에 **목이 잠겨** 명확하게 말할 수 없었어요. 그래서 전 다시 처음부터 시작해야 했죠. 감기에 걸린 것 같아요.

이렇게 말하자:

주디: 조, 어떻게 지냈어?

조: (쉰 목소리로) 나쁘지 않아. 고마워.

주디: 어머, 근데 네 목소리 엉망인데! 괜찮은 거 맞아?

조: 응, 방금 진짜 매운 카레를 먹었는데, 그래서 **목이 잠겼어.** 몇 분 지나면 괜찮을 거야.

There is no reason why* anyone should drink alcohol and then drive a car. That's **a no-brainer**! It's stupid and dangerous. It's absolutely the wrong thing to do, but so many people still do it!

IN A REAL CONVERSATION

Ritchie: Tommy was banned from driving because the police stopped him and breathalysed* him. He had only drunk one beer. I think being banned is a bit harsh*.

Sarah: No way! Drinking and driving can kill people. People shouldn't be allowed to drive at all if they are going to drink alcohol. That's **a no-brainer**!

당연한 것
a no-brainer
Com/Inf

Something very easy or obvious that needs little thought. It is so easy/obvious that you don't need to use your brain.
아주 쉽거나 명백해서 거의 생각이 필요 없는 것, 머리를 쓸 필요가 없을 정도로 쉽거나 당연한 것

이건 뇌가 필요 없어!

술 먹고 운전하는 건 위험해!

누구든지 아무런 이유도 없이 술을 마시고 차를 운전해서는 안 됩니다. 그건 **당연한 것**이죠! 그건 어리석고 위험해요. 잘못된 일이라는 게 분명한데도, 여전히 많은 사람이 음주 운전을 해요!

* reason why ~하는 이유

이렇게 말하자:

리치: 경찰이 토미를 세우고 음주 측정을 했는데, 운전면허를 정지당했어. 겨우 맥주 한 잔 마셨을 뿐인데, 나는 면허 정지는 좀 가혹하다고 생각해.

사라: 말도 안 돼! 음주 운전은 사람을 죽일 수도 있어. 술을 마실 거면 운전하는 것을 절대 허용해서는 안 돼. 그건 **당연한 거**야!

* breathalyzed [AM]   * harsh 가혹한(= cruel, severe)

A shotgun wedding

A long time ago, '**shotgun weddings**' were a real thing! The father of a pregnant, unmarried girl would take his gun and use it to force the responsible male to marry and take care of his daughter. I'm glad that doesn't happen anymore.

IN A REAL CONVERSATION

Hailey: Toby! I just heard you are getting married to Angela. That was very sudden, but congratulations anyway!

Toby: Ah, ummm, thanks. Well, it's a little embarrassing. It's **a shotgun wedding**.

Hailey: Hahaha! That's hilarious! You should have been* more careful, but anyway, I'm really happy for you both!

006. MP3

속도위반 결혼
a shotgun wedding
Com/Inf

A marriage that is the result of an unplanned pregnancy

계획하지 않은 임신으로 인한 결혼 (오래전 미국에서 딸이 혼전에 임신하면 아버지가 총을 들고 남자에게 찾아가 딸을 책임지라고 했던 것에서 유래했다고 한다)

엽총 결혼

오래전, '**엽총 결혼**'은 글자 그대로였어요! 혼전 임신한 여자의 아버지가 총을 가져가서 책임이 있는 남자에게 결혼해서 딸을 돌보게 하려고 그걸 사용했죠. 더 이상 그런 일이 일어나지 않아서 다행이에요.

이렇게 말하자:

헤일리: 토비! 나 방금 네가 안젤라와 결혼한다는 얘기를 들었어. 너무 갑작스럽긴 하지만 축하해!

토비: 오, 음… 고마워. 있잖아, 음, 조금 당황스러운 게, 그게 **속도위반 결혼**이야.

헤일리: 하하하! 진짜 웃겨! 네가 조금 더 주의를 했어야지, 하지만 어쨌거나, 너희 두 사람 정말 잘됐다!

* should have p.p. ~했어야 했다(그런데 안 했다)

A skeleton in the closet

A politician was removed from his position yesterday when he was found to have **a skeleton in his closet**. He had been arrested 12 times for drink driving when he was younger. He's lucky to be alive after drinking and driving so many times!

IN A REAL CONVERSATION

Carl: Have you heard that Alison broke up with* her boyfriend?

Sally: Yeah, I heard that she discovered that he had **a skeleton in his closet**.

Carl: Right! She found out that he is divorced from another woman and they have three kids!

007. MP3

감추고 싶은 비밀
**a skeleton
in one's closet**
Com/Inf

A dark secret someone has which, if revealed, would have a negative effect on that person
누군가 가지고 있는 어두운 비밀로. 폭로된다면 그 사람에게 부정적인 영향을 줄 수 있는 것 (옷장 속에 몰래 시체를 감춰두고 시간이 지나 해골이 된 상황을 감추고 싶은 비밀에 비유한 것이다)

A skeleton in the closet

옷장 속에 해골

어제 한 정치인이 **감추고 싶은 비밀**이 드러나 자리에서 물러났습니다. 그 사람이 젊었을 때 음주 운전으로 12번이나 체포된 적이 있었던 거죠. 그렇게 음주 운전을 많이 하고도 살아 있다니 운은 좋네요!

이렇게 말하자:

칼: 앨리슨이 남자친구와 헤어졌다는 거 들었어?

샐리: 응, 그 남자한테 **엄청난 비밀**이 있었던 걸 알게 됐다고 하더라구.

칼: 맞아! 그 남자가 다른 여자랑 이혼했고 애가 셋이 있다는 걸 알아냈지!

*break up with ~와 헤어지다

A slap in the face

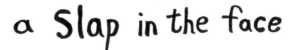

I used to* have a good friend called Toby. We used to hang out* together a lot and I used to help him with his university assignments, but then I found out that he was secretly meeting my girlfriend! That was **a** real **slap in the face.** I never spoke to him or my ex-girlfriend again.

IN A REAL CONVERSATION

Wife: I was demoted* today and replaced by a new university graduate.

Husband: What? No way! You've worked so hard in that job. That's **a** real **slap in the face**!

008. MP3

모욕적인 행동
a slap in the face
Com/Inf

A shocking act that insults or offends someone
누군가를 모욕하거나 불쾌하게 하는 충격적인 행동

a slap in the face

따귀 한 방

전 토비라는 친한 친구가 있었어요. 우린 함께 많이 놀러 다녔고 저는 걔 대학 과제를 많이 도와주곤 했지만, 저는 걔가 제 여자친구와 몰래 만나고 있다는 것을 알게 됐죠! 그건 진짜 **따귀 한 방 맞은 기분**이었어요. 전 다시는 걔나 전 여자 친구와는 말을 섞지 않았습니다.

*used to ~하곤 했다, 한때 ~했다(지금은 아니다)
*hang out 시간을 보내다, 어울려 다니다

**이렇게
말하자:**

아내: 나 오늘 좌천됐는데 갓 대학을 졸업한 사회 초년생이 내 자리로 왔어.

남편: 뭐? 말도 안 돼! 당신 진짜 그 일 열심히 했잖아. 그건 진짜 **모욕적**이야!

*demote 강등시키다, 좌천시키다(↔ promote 승진시키다)

29

A wet blanket

He's a wet blanket

I was playing football* in the park with some of my friends this morning. We were having a great time until one of my friends decided to leave. He owned the ball we were playing with and he wouldn't let us use it. He took it home with him. What **a wet blanket**!

IN A REAL CONVERSATION

Harry: Did you see Tom at the party last night? He just sat alone in the corner all night and didn't talk to anyone.

Sally: Yeah. He's always like that. He's **a real wet blanket**!

009. MP3

분위기 깨는 사람
a wet blanket
Com/Inf

A person who spoils other people's fun by not participating or because they don't like the activity
참여하지 않거나 그 활동을 좋아하지 않아서 다른 사람들의 즐거움을 망치는 사람

He's a wet blanket

쟤는
젖은 담요야

오늘 아침 저는 공원에서 친구 몇 명하고 축구를 하고 있었어요. 친구 하나가 가기로 하기 전까지는 우리는 정말 즐겁게 시간을 보내고 있었죠. 우리가 가지고 놀던 공이 그 애 것이었는데 그 앤 우리가 공을 사용하지 못하게 했어요. 공을 가지고 집에 가버렸죠. 진짜 **분위기를 깨는 애**에요!

* soccer [AM]

이렇게 말하자:

해리: 너 어젯밤 파티에서 톰 봤어? 그냥 밤새 구석에서 혼자 앉아 아무하고도 얘기를 안 하던데.

샐리: 맞아. 걔는 항상 그런 식이야. 진짜 **분위기 못 맞춰**!

Add fuel to the fire

I had a meeting with my boss today about some problems at work. I know that a few of my co-workers are leaving the company very soon, but I decided not to tell her. I didn't want to **add fuel to the fire**.

IN A REAL CONVERSATION

Liane: I saw a young boy crying in the street and his mother didn't console* him. She just shouted at him.

Anton: Really? That's terrible. Shouting at a crying child is just **adding fuel to the fire**.

010. MP3

불난 데 부채질하다.
문제를 악화시키다
add fuel to the fire
Com/Inf

To make a problem worse
문제를 악화시키다

"석유"

불에 기름을 끼얹어

오늘 회사에서 몇 가지 문제로 사장님과 회의했어요. 전 동료
몇 명이 곧 회사를 나간다는 것을 알고 있었지만, 사장님에게
말하지 않기로 결심했어요. 저는 **불난 데 부채질하는** 것을 원하지
않거든요.

**이렇게
말하자:**

리안: 남자 아이가 길에서 울고 있는 걸 봤는데 애 엄마가 아이를
달래지 않는 거야. 애한테 소리만 치더라고.

안톤: 정말? 끔찍하다. 우는 아이에게 소리 치는 것은 그냥 **불난 데
부채질하는** 거야.

*console 위로하다

Another one bites the dust

I read in the newspaper today that another politician has been sacked* for illegal money deals. It's good to see that the government has got rid of* another corrupt politician. **Another one bites the dust!**

IN A REAL CONVERSATION

Eric: The company I work for has become very successful over the last few years. Our competitors are having a hard time competing with us.

Kim: Yeah, I heard two of them went bankrupt last year, and another one went bankrupt last week. **Another one bites the dust.**

011. MP3

또 한 명이 패배하다,
죽다, 망하다
**another one
bites the dust**
Com/Inf

To fail/fall out of the competition, die.
This expression comes from the action
of falling face down onto the ground.
경쟁에서 실패하다/떨어지다, 죽다. 이 표현은 얼굴이
땅바닥에 떨어지는 동작에서 나왔다.

"부패 정치인 파면!"

또 한 놈이 흙을 물었네

전 오늘 또 다른 정치인이 불법적인 금전 거래로 파면당했다는
것을 신문에서 읽었어요. 정부가 부패한 정치인을 하나 더
제거하는 것을 봐서 좋네요. **그 정치인은 패배한 거죠!**

* fired [AM]
* get rid of ~을 처리하다, ~을 제거하다

**이렇게
말하자:**

에릭: 내가 일하는 회사는 지난 몇 년 동안 아주 잘되고 있어.
경쟁사들이 우리하고 경쟁하는 데에 어려움을 겪고 있지.

킴: 응, 난 작년에 그중 두 곳이 파산했다고 들었어. 그리고 다른
한 곳은 지난주에 파산했고, **또 하나가 망했지.**

Ants in your pants

Young kids can be very excitable. My son loves Christmas day. He loves getting presents from Santa. On Christmas Eve, he is so excited and has **ants in his pants**. He can't sit down for more than a few minutes.

IN A REAL CONVERSATION

Teacher: Tom! We are about to* start your maths test. Why are you moving around in your seat so much? Have you got **ants in your pants**?

Student: No, miss. I'm just really nervous about this test.

012. MP3

안절부절못함
ants in
one's pants
Com/Inf

Not being able to sit still because you are anxious or excited about something. This is an old-fashioned but humorous expression.

뭔가에 대해 불안하거나 초조해서 앉아 있지 못함. 구식이지만 재미있는 표현이다.

바지 속에 개미들

어린애들은 매우 흥분하기 쉽습니다. 제 아들은 크리스마스를 정말 좋아해요. 산타한테 선물 받는 것을 좋아하죠. 크리스마스 전날에 그 애는 너무 흥분해서 **안절부절못해요**. 단 몇 분도 못 앉아 있죠.

이렇게 말하자:

선생님: 톰! 우리 지금 수학 시험을 막 시작하려고 해. 왜 의자에 가만히 앉아 있지 못하니? **바지 속에 개미들**이라도 있는 거야?

학생: 아니요, 선생님. 전 그냥 이 시험 때문에 진짜 긴장하고 있는 거예요.

* be about to 막 ~를 하려는 참이다

013

As quick as a flash

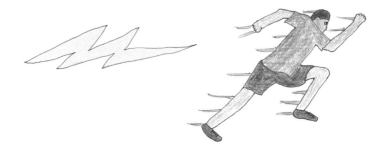

I love spicy food. When my friend called me to invite me to an Indian restaurant for lunch, I was out the door **as quick as a flash** to meet her. Next time, I will treat* her to some spicy Korean chicken stew!

George: Have you had lunch?

Lisa: Yes. I went to a very nice Vietnamese restaurant. The food was fantastic, the staff were very friendly and the waitress brought the food to our table **as quick as a flash**!

013. MP3

신속하게
as quick as a flash
Com/Inf

Very quickly
매우 빠르게

As quick as a flash

번개처럼 빠르게

전 매운 음식을 정말 좋아해요. 친구가 전화해서 점심으로 저를 인도 식당에 초대했을 때, **잽싸게** 문밖으로 나가서 그 친구를 만났죠. 다음엔, 제가 친구한테 매운 한국식 닭볶음탕을 한턱낼 거예요!

*treat 대접하다, 한턱내다

이렇게 말하자:

조지: 너 점심 먹었어?

리사: 응. 정말 괜찮은 베트남 식당에 갔어. 음식이 정말 맛있었어. 직원도 매우 친절하고, 종업원이 음식을 우리 테이블에 **신속하게** 가져다주었어!

014

At the eleventh hour

It's my wife's birthday today. I've been thinking about getting her a present all week, but I've just been SO busy. Luckily though, I managed to* rush out and get a beautiful bracelet an hour ago, just **at the eleventh hour!**

IN A REAL CONVERSATION

Doctor 1: How is your kidney patient? I heard that he was in a really bad way*.

Doctor 2: Yes, he was. Luckily though, we found a kidney donor **at the eleventh hour** and now he's recovering from a very successful transplant operation!

막판에
at the eleventh hour
Com/Inf

014. MP3

At the last moment or almost too late
마지막 순간에 또는 거의 너무 늦게

"휴우"
"만세!"
"안 돼!"

열한 번째 시간에

오늘은 제 아내 생일이에요. 한 주 내내 선물을 사려고 생각했지만, 너무나 바빠서 그러질 못했어요. 그래도 다행히도 서둘러 나가 한 시간 전에 간신히 아름다운 팔찌를 샀어요. 딱 **마지막 순간에**요!

* manage to 간신히 ~하다, 어떻게든 ~해내다

**이렇게
말하자:**

의사 1: 당신의 신장 환자는 어때요? 그 환자가 정말 안 좋은 상태라고 들었어요.

의사 2: 네, 그랬죠. 운 좋게도 **마지막 순간에** 신장 기증자를 찾아서, 아주 성공적으로 이식 수술을 하고 지금 회복 중이에요!

* in a bad way 위험한 상태로, 중태로

015

Button your lip

Button
your
lip

My friend made me really angry in the pub last night. He kept telling sexist and racist jokes. I got so angry that I told him to button his lip, and left the pub. I'm not going to meet him again unless he apologises*!

Jerry: I went to a restaurant a few days ago, and on the table next to me, a couple was having an argument. They were being really loud and disturbing everyone in the restaurant.

Cathy: Really? So what happened next?

Jerry: Well, I really wanted to say something, but I decided to just **button my lip**. The manager soon went over and told them to be quiet.

입을 다물다
button one's lip
Com/Inf

To say nothing or stop talking. This is very informal and if you say it to someone, it's the same as "shut up!".

아무 말도 하지 않거나 말하는 것을 멈추다. 이 표현은 아주 비격식적이라서, 이렇게 말하면 "입 닥쳐"라고 하는 것과 같다. (비슷한 표현: bite one's lip, zip one's lip, hold one's tongue)

Button your lip

입술에
단추를 채워

친구가 지난밤 술집에서 절 정말 화나게 했어요. 그는 계속해서 성차별적이고 인종차별적인 농담을 했죠. 전 정말 화가 나서 걔한테 **입 닥치**라고 말했어요. 그리고 술집을 나갔어요. 걔가 사과하기 전까진 걔를 만나지 않을 거예요!

* apologizes [AM]

이렇게
말하자:

제리: 며칠 전에 식당에 갔는데, 내 옆 식탁에 한 커플이 다투고 있는 거야. 진짜 큰 소리를 내면서 식당 안에 있는 모두를 방해하고 있었어.

케시: 정말? 그래서 다음에 어떻게 됐어?

제리: 음, 한 소리 하고 싶었지만, 그냥 **입을 다물기로** 했어. 지배인이 바로 가서 조용히 하라고 말했거든.

016

Better not

My work colleague is a smoker and sometimes we take a break together outside our work building. He was just about to light his cigarette this morning when I noticed some containers of fuel behind him! I told him that he had **better not** smoke there.

Wife: Do you think we should tell the kids that we might be moving to Australia?

Husband: **Better not**. Let's wait until it's completely confirmed. They'll just be disappointed if it falls through*.

하지 않는 것이 좋다
better not
Com/Inf

016. MP3

This expression is used to advise someone that they should not do a particular thing.

이 표현은 특정 행위를 하지 말아야 한다고 충고할 때 사용한다.

- 여기서 담배 피워도 돼요?
- 음… 안 피우는 게 좋을 텐데요!

제 동료는 흡연자인데 가끔 회사 건물 밖으로 나가 함께 휴식을 취합니다. 오늘 아침 그 사람이 담배에 막 불을 붙이려고 하는데, 뒤에 연료통이 있는 것을 제가 알아챘어요! 전 거기서 담배 피우지 **않는 게 좋겠다**고 했죠.

이렇게 말하자:

아내: 애들한테 호주로 이사 갈 수도 있다고 말해야 한다고 생각해?
남편: **안 하는 것이 좋겠어.** 완전히 정해질 때까지 기다리자. 취소된다면 애들은 바로 실망할 거야.

* fall through 실패로 끝나다(= come to nothing, fail)

45

017

Better the devil you know

A new mechanic has started a business in my neighbourhood* and he is much cheaper than my current mechanic. My current mechanic is not very friendly and his prices are high, but he always does a very good job. I think I'll just stay with my current mechanic. **Better the devil you know!**

Marnie: I've been offered a job with a better salary, but I'm not sure if I should take it. I really like my current job and all my coworkers. I really don't know much about the new job I've been offered.

Harry: Well, if you're happy in your current job, I don't think you should change. **Better the devil you know!**

017. MP3

구관이 명관이다
better the devil you know
Com/Inf

It is better to deal with a person or situation that you are familiar with than to take a risk with something or someone that you are not familiar with.
익숙하지 않은 사람이나 상황을 대하며 위험을 감수하는 것보다 익숙한 것을 다루는 것이 낫다 (완래 표현은 Better the devil you know then the devil you don't. 모르는 악마보다 아는 악마가 낫다)

아는 악마가 낫지!
"안녕!"

새 정비사가 우리 동네에 사업을 시작했는데, 지금 정비사보다 훨씬 저렴해요. 제 현재 정비사는 그렇게 친절하지도 않은 데다 비용도 많이 들어요. 하지만 그는 항상 일을 잘합니다. 전 그냥 현재 정비사와 함께하려고 합니다. **구관이 명관이니까요!**

* neighborhood [AM]

이렇게 말하자:

마니: 내가 더 나은 급여로 일 제의를 받았는데, 받아들여야 할지 확신이 안 서. 지금 하는 일과 동료들이 정말 좋고, 새로 제의받은 일에 대해선 잘 모르거든.

해리: 음, 네가 현재 직업에 만족한다면 바꿀 필요는 없을 것 같아. **구관이 명관이잖아!**

018

Between you and me

Between you and me...

A colleague of mine has asked me to invest money in his new business, but between you and me, I don't think it's a good idea to do business with him. I've heard that he has cheated a few people in the past in order to get money.

Emma: Have you heard? Harry is moving to South Korea to be an English teacher!

Boyle: Really? I don't think he's doing the right thing.

Emma: Really? Why?

Boyle: Well... **Between you and me**, he's not a very friendly guy and I don't think he's got the right personality to be a teacher.

018. MP3

우리끼리 얘긴데
**between
you and me**
Com/Inf

What I am about to say should be kept secret.
내가 말하려고 하는 것은 비밀로 해야 한다.

Between you and me...

너와 나의 사이에…

제 동료 하나가 자기 새 사업에 돈을 투자해달라고 부탁을 했어요. 하지만 **우리끼리 얘긴데**, 그 사람하고 사업을 하는 것은 좋은 생각이 아닌 것 같아요. 그 사람이 예전에 돈을 구하려고 몇 사람한테 사기 쳤다고 들었거든요.

이렇게
말하자:

엠마: 너 들었어? 해리가 한국으로 이사할 거래, 영어 교사가 되려고!
보일: 정말? 흠, 잘하고 있는 게 아닌 거 같은데.
엠마: 정말? 왜?
보일: 음… **우리끼리 이야기지만**, 걔는 그다지 친근한 사람은 아니라서, 난 걔가 교사가 되기에 적합한 성격이라고 생각하지 않아.

019

Blow by blow

I witnessed a crime last night. I saw a man attack another man in a dark alleyway. Luckily, he wasn't seriously injured. I went to the police station and gave them a **blow by blow** account of* what I saw. I hope they catch him!

English teacher 1: What is a good way to make a students talk more, without having to keep asking questions?

English teacher 2: Well, something I do often is tell my student to give me a **blow by blow** account of everything he/she did on the previous weekend.

상세하게
blow by blow
Com/Inf

A detailed description of an event, in the correct time order
정확한 시간 순서에 따른, 사건에 대한 자세한 묘사

한 방 한 방

전 지난밤에 범죄를 목격했어요. 어두운 골목길에서 한 남자가 다른 남자를 공격하는 것을 봤죠. 다행히 그는 심각하게 다치지는 않았어요. 전 경찰서에 가서 제가 보았던 것을 **상세하게** 설명했어요. 경찰이 그 남자를 잡았으면 좋겠어요!

* give an account of ~을 설명하다

이렇게
말하자:

영어 교사 1: 학생들이 말을 더 많이 하도록 만드는 좋은 방법이 뭐가 있을까? 계속 질문만 하는 것 말고.

영어 교사 2: 글쎄, 내가 자주 하는 것은, 학생들에게 주말에 했던 모든 것을 **상세하게** 말해달라고 하는 거야.

020

Blood is thicker than water

My best friend got into* a fist fight with my brother. It was a difficult choice to make but **blood is thicker than water**, so I helped my brother. Sadly, I have lost a friend.

Jade: My best friend had a big argument with my sister last night.

Joe: Oh no! What did you do?

Jade: It was a really stupid disagreement, but I had to take my sister's side*. After all, **blood is thicker than water**.

피는 물보다 진하다,
팔은 안으로 굽는다
blood is thicker than water
Com/Inf

020. MP3

Family relationships are more important than other relationships.
다른 관계보다 가족 관계가 더 중요하다.

피는 물보다 진하다

친한 친구가 제 동생과 주먹다짐했어요. 선택하는 게 어려웠지만
피는 물보다 진하니까, 전 동생을 도왔어요.
슬프게도 전 친구를 잃었죠.

* get into ~을 시작하다, (~한 상태에) 처하다

이렇게
말하자:

제이드: 내 절친이랑 내 동생이 지난밤에 크게 싸웠어.
조: 오 저런! 넌 어떻게 했어?
제이드: 음, 그게 정말 어리석은 싸움이었지만, 하지만 난 동생 편을
들어야 했어. 결국, **팔은 안으로 굽는 거잖아.**

* take one's side ~의 편을 들다

Two of my friends had a big argument about politics, but they're good friends and they have had disagreements before. The bad feelings will soon **blow over** and they will be friends again.

Shawn: The virus spreading around the country is really worrying everyone.

Cheryl: Yeah. It's a troubling time, but I'm sure it's just a matter of time until it **blows over**.

잠잠해지다
blow over
Con/Inf

021. MP3

To fade away. If a bad situation blows over, people stop worrying about it.

사라지다 나쁜 상황이 blow over한다고 하면, 사람들이 그에 대한 걱정을 그만한다는 뜻이다.

문제가 불려
날아갈 때까지
기다려

제 친구 둘이 정치에 대해서 크게 논쟁을 벌였지만, 걔들은 좋은 친구고 전에도 의견 충돌은 있었어요. 나쁜 감정은 곧 **사그라들고** 걔들은 다시 좋은 친구가 될 거예요.

이렇게
말하자:

선: 바이러스가 전국에 퍼지는 것은 진짜 모두에게 걱정이야.

셰릴: 응. 힘든 시기지만 그게 **잠잠해지기**까지 단지 시간 문제라고 봐.

Breathe down my neck

I've just started a new job, and I love it. I don't think my boss trusts me to do my work correctly yet, though*. He's always breathing down my neck! I hope he leaves me alone soon!

Andy: My wife really drove me crazy last night!

Monica: Why?

Andy: Well, she's on a diet. While I was cooking dinner, she was **breathing down my neck** the whole time. She was checking that I wasn't using any fatty ingredients. She's working late tonight, so I'm going to order delivery fried chicken!

022. MP3

눈에 불을 켜고 지켜보다
breathe down one's neck
Com/Inf

To follow someone around and watch everything they do

누군가의 곁에 맴돌면서 무엇을 하는지 사사건건 지켜보다

내 목에 숨을
내뿜고 있어

전 새 일을 막 시작했는데, 이 일이 정말 좋아요. 하지만 제
상사는 아직 제가 일을 제대로 한다고 믿지 않는 것 같아요.
항상 **눈에 불을 켜고 지켜보고** 있거든요. 상사가 빨리 저를
혼자 내버려 두면 좋겠어요!

* though (문장 끝에서) 하지만, 그렇지만

이렇게
말하자:

앤디: 내 아내가 지난 밤에 날 미쳐버리게 했어!

모니카: 왜?

앤디: 음, 아내가 다이어트 중이거든. 내가 저녁을 하는 동안, 내내 **등
뒤에서 지켜보는** 거야. 내가 기름진 재료라도 사용하진 않는지
확인하려고! 아내가 오늘 밤늦게까지 일하니, 난 후라이드
치킨을 배달시킬 거야!

Bringing home the bacon

Times have changed a lot. In the past, it was usually the man in the household who made money to support his family. Nowadays, more and more women are bringing home the bacon.

IN A REAL CONVERSATION

Dino: I'm quitting my job at the end of the month. My wife makes more money than me and she wants to work, so I'm going to be a househusband*. I'm going to stay at home and take care of the kids.

Rachel: Cool! It doesn't matter who does what, as long as someone is **bringing home the bacon**, and someone is taking care of the kids.

023. MP3

생활비를 벌다
bring home the bacon
Com/Inf

To earn money, particularly for your family; to be successful, especially financially successful. In this expression, the word 'bacon' means 'money'.

당신의 가족을 위해 집을 마련하기 위해, 특히 재정적으로 성공하려고 돈을 벌다. 이 표현에서 베이컨은 돈을 나타낸다.

집에 베이컨을
가져가는

시간은 많은 것을 변화시키죠. 과거에는 가족을 부양하기 위해 가정에서 돈을 버는 것은 주로 남자였습니다. 요즘에는 점점 더 많은 여자가 **생활비를 벌고** 있어요.

디노: 난 이달 말에 직장을 그만두려고 해. 아내가 나보다 많이 버는 데다가, 일하고 싶어 해. 그래서 난 가사를 돌보는 남편이 되려고. 내가 집에 있으면서 애들을 돌볼 거야.

레이첼: 멋지다! 누가 뭘 하는지는 상관없어, 누군가가 애들을 돌보고 있는 한은 누군가가 **생계를 꾸려** 나가야지.

* househusband 가사와 육아를 전담하는 아빠(= stay at home dad)

A lot of people have a long **bucket list**. There are only two things on my **bucket list**. I want to marry a beautiful woman and make a million pounds. Nothing is impossible!

Jenny: What are you doing?

Ross: I'm tired of my boring life, so I'm writing a **bucket list**.

Jenny: Oh, what's on the list so far?

Ross: I want to own a Ferrari, buy a house near a beach and learn how to play the piano.

024. MP3

죽기 전에 할 일
bucket list
Com/Inf

A list of experiences or achievements that a person wants to complete during their lifetime

한 사람이 평생 이루기를 원하는 경험 또는 업적
(이 말은 Kick the bucket(양동이를 걷어차다 → 죽다)에서 유래했는데, bucket(양동이)과 list(목록)가 합쳐져 '죽기 전에 할 것들'을 뜻하게 되었다)

피라미드 보기, 문신하기, 돌고래랑 수영하기, 유럽 여행하기, 번지점프하기, 스카이다이빙하기

See the pyramids
Swim with dolphins
Bungee jump
get a tattoo
visit Europe
SKY dive

My bucket list

"나의 버킷리스트"

많은 사람은 긴 **버킷 리스트**를 가지고 있습니다. 제 **버킷 리스트**에는 두 개뿐이에요. 아름다운 여자와 결혼하는 것, 그리고 100만 파운드를 모으는 거죠. 불가능한 것은 없어요!

이렇게 말하자:

제니: 뭐 하는 중이야?

로스: 난 내 지루한 삶에 싫증 나. 그래서 **죽기 전에 할 일**을 적고 있어.

제니: 오, 지금까지 목록에 뭐가 있어?

로스: 페라리를 갖고 싶고, 해변의 집을 사고, 그리고 피아노 치는 법을 배우고 싶어.

025

Call it a day

It's starting to rain

yeah let's call it a day

My friend and I had a great time fishing in the river yesterday, but then it started to rain, so we decided to call it a day and went to the pub for a beer. We had a better time in the bar than we did at the river!

· ·

IN A REAL CONVERSATION

Businessperson 1:	How's your new company doing? You started it about a year ago, right?
Businessperson 2:	Actually, it's been over two years, but sadly it's not making any money. I'm seriously thinking about **calling it a day**.

025. MP3

그만하기로 하다
call it a day
Com/Inf

To stop doing something because you do not want to do it anymore or because you have done enough

더 이상 하고 싶지 않거나 충분히 했기 때문에, 그만하다

It's starting to rain

yeah, let's call it a day

비가 오기 시작했어
아, 여기까지를
하루로 부르자구

제 친구와 저는 어제 강에서 낚시하며 좋은 시간을 보내고 있었어요. 하지만 비가 오기 시작해서, 우리는 **그만하기로 하고** 맥주를 마시러 술집에 갔어요. 우리는 강에서보다 술집에서 더 좋은 시간을 보냈죠!

이렇게
말하자:

사업가 1: 새 회사는 어때요? 1년쯤 전에 시작하셨죠?
사업가 2: 실은 2년이 넘었지만, 불행히도 돈을 전혀 못 벌고 있어요. **그만두는 것**을 진지하게 생각하고 있어요.

026

Cause a scene

My husband has just caused a big scene in a department store. We took a pair of jeans to be exchanged, but the staff were too busy to talk to us, so my husband got angry and started shouting! Everyone was watching us.

Tommy: My neighbour* is driving me crazy! He keeps parking his car in my parking space.

Melody: Well, it's better that you don't **cause a scene**. It would probably be better to just politely ask him to stop doing it.

소란 피우다
cause a scene
Com/Inf

To create a loud disturbance or display in a public area (often as a result of anger), which draws attention from the people in that area

공공장소에서 큰 소리로 소란을 일으키거나 감정 표현을 해대주로 분노해서) 거기 있는 사람들의 관심을 끄다 (비슷한 표현: create a scene, make a scene)

- 난 기분이 안 좋다고!
- 저 남자 안 좋은 상황을 만들고 있네

"고객 불만 센터"

제 남편이 방금 백화점에서 큰 **소란을 피웠어요**. 우리는 바지 한 벌을 교환하려고 가져갔는데, 직원이 너무 바빠 우리와 말을 할 수 없었어요. 그랬더니, 제 남편이 화가 나서 소리를 치기 시작하는 거예요! 모두가 우리를 쳐다보고 있었죠.

이렇게
말하자:

토미: 이웃이 나를 미쳐버리게 해! 계속해서 내 주차 공간에 자기 차를 대는 거야.

멜로디: 음, **소란을 피우지** 않는 편이 나아. 네가 정중히 그러지 말라고 부탁하는 게 아마 더 나을 수 있어.

* neighbor [AM]

Chasing
rainbows

Tommy used to be good at football when he was a child. Recently, he started wondering if he should try to become a professional football player. Then he realized that he was just chasing rainbows. After all, he is 50 years old now!

Julie: I heard that Toby's taking acting lessons. He really wants to become a Hollywood actor.

Ruben: Ha! He's been like that all his life. He has wanted to be a rock star, an astronaut, and the president! He's never stopped **chasing rainbows**.

027. MP3

뜬 구름을 좇다,
허황된 꿈을 꾸다
chase rainbows
Com/Inf

To constantly try to achieve things that
are unrealistic, impossible or unlikely to
happen

Chasing
rainbows

무지개를 따라가는

토미는 어렸을 때 축구를 잘했어요. 최근에, 그는 프로 축구
선수가 되려고 해봐야 하는지 생각하기 시작했어요. 그런 다음
자기가 **뜬구름을 좇고 있다**는 것을 깨달았죠. 어쨌든, 그는 지금
50살이거든요!

이렇게
말하자:

줄리: 난 토비가 연기 수업을 받고 있다고 들었어. 걔는 정말
헐리우드 배우가 되고 싶어 해.

루벤: 해! 걘 평생 그런 식이야. 록스타가 되고 싶다더니, 우주비행사,
그리고 대통령이 되고 싶어 해왔지. 걔는 **뜬구름을 좇는** 것을
절대 그만두지 않아.

028

Come up roses

I've got a new job! Now I can start saving money to buy a new home. And my parents have just bought me a new car. Everything is coming up roses. I hope the good luck continues!

Berry:	How's it going, Liz?
Liz:	Fantastic! My boss has given me a pay rise, my boyfriend bought me a new phone and I'm going on holiday to the UK next month!
Berry:	Wow, everything is really **coming up roses** for you! Lucky you!

잘 되어가다
come up roses
Com/Inf

Things are going well and happening successfully.

모든 것이
장미로
피어나고 있다

저에게 새로운 일자리가 생겼어요! 지금 새집을 사려고 돈을 모으기 시작했어요. 그리고 부모님이 새 차를 사주셨죠. 모든 것이 **순조로워요**. 행운이 계속되면 좋겠어요!

이렇게
말하자:

배리: 리즈, 요즘 어때?

리즈: 정말 좋아! 사장이 급여를 인상해 줬고, 남자친구는 새 폰을 사줬고, 다음 달에는 영국으로 휴가를 갈 거야.

배리: 와, 모든 것이 정말 너한테 **잘 되어가네**! 행운을 빌어!

029

Cost a bomb

I'm planning to propose to my girlfriend tonight!
I bought a diamond engagement ring for her last
week. It cost a bomb, so she'd better say "Yes".
If she says "No", I'm going to get a refund!

Frank: I've always wanted a Rolex watch, but they
cost a bomb.

Sue: Well, if you REALLY want one, I guess you'll
just have to start doing more overtime at
work to make some extra money.

큰돈이 들다
cost a bomb
Com/Inf

To be very expensive

"다이아몬드 반지"

이건 폭탄 같은
거금이 들어

전 오늘 저녁 여자친구에게 청혼하려고 해요! 지난주에
여자친구를 위해 다이아몬드 약혼반지를 샀어요. **큰돈이 들었죠**.
그래서 여자친구가 승낙하면 좋겠어요. 만약에 여자친구가
"싫어"라고 한다면, 환불하려고요!

이렇게
말하자:

프랭크: 난 항상 롤렉스 시계를 원했지만 그건 **큰돈이 들지**.

수: 음, 네가 정말 하나 갖고 싶다면, 추가로 돈을 좀 모으기 위해
회사에서 초과 근무를 좀 더 시작해야 할 거야.

030

Could be worse

Could
be
worse!

you
could have
been hurt!

My car broke down and burst into flames yesterday, so I have to buy a new car. It's going to cost a lot of money. It **could** have **been worse**. At least I wasn't injured!

. . . .

IN A REAL CONVERSATION

Zack: Someone stole my wallet yesterday!

Kelly: Oh, no!

Zack: They took all my cash, but I guess it **could** have **been worse**. I found it later and all of my credit cards were still inside it.

Kelly: Wow! You were lucky that you got your cards back.

그만하길 다행이다
could be worse
Com/Inf

This expression is used to describe that a situation that could have had a worse result than it actually did.

이 표현은 실제보다 더 나쁜 결과였을 수 있었던 상황을 나타낼 때 사용된다.

네가 다칠 수도 있었다고!

더 나쁠 수도 있었어!

어제 제 차가 망가지더니 불꽃이 터져서, 새 차를 사야 해요. 돈은 많이 들겠지만요. **그만하길 다행이에요.** 최소한 전 다치지 않았으니까요!

이렇게 말하자:

잭: 누군가 어제 내 지갑을 훔쳐 갔어!
켈리: 오, 저런!
잭: 현금을 다 가져갔지만 **그만하길 다행이었던** 것 같아. 지갑을 나중에 찾았는데 신용카드는 그 안에 다 있었어.
켈리: 와! 신용카드는 돌려받았으니 다행이다.

031

Cross the line

Harry was often late for work, but his boss didn't reprimand* him because he was a hard worker. One day, he really crossed the line. He arrived at work drunk! His boss wouldn't tolerate it. He sacked* Harry immediately.

Boss:	You are 30 minutes late!
Employee:	Sorry, boss.
Boss:	That is the third time this week.
Employee:	Sorry, boss.
Boss:	Well, be careful. Don't **cross the line**. This is your last warning.
Employee:	Sorry, boss.

031. MP3

선을 넘다.
도를 넘다, 지나치다
cross the line
Com/Inf

To do something that is unacceptable

선을 넘지 마시오

해리는 종종 회사에 지각했지만, 사장님은 그를 질책하지
않았어요. 왜냐하면 그는 열심히 일하는 사람이거든요.
어느 날, 해리는 **도를 넘었어요**. 술에 취해서 출근한 거죠.
사장님도 더 이상 참지 못했던 모양이에요. 해리를 그 자리에서
해고하더라고요.

reprimand 질책하다
fired [AM]

이렇게
말하자:

상사: 30분이나 지각이네요!
직원: 죄송합니다.
상사: 이번 주에 벌써 세 번째예요. 음, 조심하세요.
직원: 죄송합니다.
상사: **선을 넘지** 마세요. 이번이 마지막 경고입니다.
직원: 죄송합니다.

Tom used to be a very good student. But recently he has been hanging out with* some troublemakers* after school. The police have warned him three times for causing trouble. He's just **digging his own grave**. He needs to be more careful.

IN A REAL CONVERSATION

Tina:	I'm going to get another credit card.
Dexter:	You've already got about seven! Do you really need another one?
Tina:	I want this one because it gives me good air miles.
Dexter:	Well, it sounds like you're just giving yourself more debt. I think you're **digging your own grave**!

032. MP3

제 무덤을 파다
dig one's own grave
Com/Inf

To do something that causes you harm, sometimes serious harm

당신에게 뭔가 해로운 것, 때로는 심각한 해가 되는 것을 하다

자기 무덤 파기
"내가 잠들다"

톰은 매우 좋은 학생이었어요. 하지만 최근에는 방과 후에 문제아들하고 어울리고 있어요. 경찰은 그에게 문제를 일으킨 것에 대해 세 번을 경고했죠. 톰은 **제 무덤을 파고** 있어요. 개는 좀 더 조심할 필요가 있어요.

*hang out with ~와 시간을 보내다, ~와 어울려 지내다
*troublemaker 말썽꾼, 사고뭉치

**이렇게
말하자:**

티나: 난 신용카드 하나 더 만들까 해.
덱스터: 너 이미 일곱 개쯤 있잖아! 정말 하나 더 필요한 거야?
티나: 이게 항공 마일리지가 좋아서 갖고 싶어.
덱스터: 글쎄, 너는 그냥 더 많은 빚을 지고 있는 것 같은데, 난 네가 네 **무덤을 파고** 있다고 생각해!

033

Dish the dirt

The Daily Times newspaper has been publishing personal information about a lot of famous pop stars and actors. Most countries have at least one tabloid newspaper that likes to **dish the dirt** on famous people. A lot of people actually enjoy that kind of gossip!

IN A REAL CONVERSATION

Dick: Hey Harry, I've got some scandalous gossip about the Chief of Police. We can blackmail* him!

Harry: Go on, **dish the dirt**.

Dick: Okay, but let's go somewhere quiet!

험담하다
dish the dirt
Com/Inf

033. MP3

To reveal or spread scandalous
information or gossip
추문을 담은 정보나 소문을 드러내거나 퍼뜨리다 (여기서
dirt(먼지)는 사람에 대한 부정적인 정보를 말하며 dish는
'담다, 내놓다'라는 뜻이므로, 결국 접시에 음식을 담아 내
놓듯이 남에 대한 험담을 꺼내놓는다는 뜻이 된다)

- 비밀 정보를
  갖고 있소
- 좋소… 더러운
  것을 담아보시오!

「데일리 타임즈」는 많은 팝스타와 배우들의 개인 정보를 싣고
있습니다. 대부분의 나라에는 유명인을 **험담하기**를 좋아하는
타블로이드 신문이 한 개는 있어요. 많은 사람이 사실 그런
종류의 소문을 즐기는 거죠!

**이렇게
말하자:**

딕: 이봐 해리, 경찰청장에 관한 추문이 있어. 우린 그자를
    협박할 수 있어!

해리: 계속해 봐, **뒷소문** 말이야.

딕: 좋아, 하지만 조용한 곳으로 가자고!

*blackmail 협박하다, 갈취하다

034

Don't paint them all with the same brush

One stereotype of lawyers is that they are dishonest and lie a lot, but I **don't** think it's fair* to **paint them all with the same brush**. I'm sure a lot of lawyers are honest and caring.

IN A REAL CONVERSATION

Claire: I don't like politicians. They never keep their promises.

Sheldon: Well, I know how you feel, but you shouldn**'t paint them all with the same brush**. I'm sure a lot of them really try to do their best.

싸잡아 보지 마라

Don't paint them all with the same brush
Com/Inf

Don't unfairly judge someone because you are basing your view on similar people or group, of whom you have a bad opinion.

당신이 나쁜 견해를 가지고 있는 다른 사람이나 집단에 대해 당신의 견해를 근거로 해서 불공평하게 판단하지 마라.
(비슷한 표현: Don't tar someone all with the same brush.)

그들을 모두
같은 색으로
칠하지 마!

변호사에 대한 고정관념 중 하나는 정직하지 않고 거짓말을 많이 한다는 것입니다만, 전 **싸잡아 보는 건** 옳지 **않다**고 생각해요. 전 많은 변호사가 정직하고 배려가 깊다고 확신해요.

*fair 공평한, 타당한

**이렇게
말하자:**

클레어: 난 정치인들을 안 좋아해. 그들은 결코 약속을 지키지 않아.

쉘던: 글쎄, 네가 어떻게 느끼는지 알지만 그렇다고 **싸잡아 봐서는 안 돼**. 난 많은 정치인이 최선을 다한다고 확신해.

035

Don't sweat the small stuff

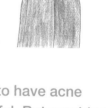

It's quite normal for teenagers to have acne problems. It can be very stressful. But most teens soon learn that it's just due to their age, and they learn **not** to **sweat the small stuff**.

IN A REAL CONVERSATION

Bob: I am worried about SO many things these days.

Jane: Everybody worries about something. It might be about your family, your job or study. Statistics show that about 40% of the things that people worry about never actually happen, so **don't sweat the small stuff**.

035. MP3

사소한 일에 너무
집착하지 마라
Don't sweat
the small stuff
Com/Inf

Don't worry about things that are not important.
중요하지 않은 것에 대해 걱정하지 마라.

- 오, 안 돼…
  여드름 났어!
- 작은 일로
  땀 흘리지 마

십대들에게 여드름 문제가 있는 것은 아주 정상이에요. 그건
십대들에게 매우 스트레스가 될 수 있죠. 하지만 대부분은
나이로 인한 것이란 걸 금방 알고, **사소한 일에 집착하지 않는
것을 배우죠.**

이렇게
말하자:

봅: 전 최근에 너무 걱정이 많았어요.

제인: 모두 뭔가를 걱정합니다. 그건 당신의 가족에 관한 것일 수
있고, 당신의 직업이나 공부에 대한 것일 수도 있죠. 통계에
따르면 사람들이 걱정하는 것의 40%는 실제로 절대 일어나지
않으니, **별거 아닌 걸로 너무 속 끓이지 마세요.**

036

Drop a bombshell

My wife and I **dropped a bombshell** on my daughter last night. We told her that we are emigrating* to Canada next month. She was shocked at first, but now she's excited about it.

IN A REAL CONVERSATION

Carl: My wife **dropped a bombshell** on me last night.
Lucy: Oh, really? What was it?
Carl: She's pregnant again!
Lucy: Wow! Congratulations!
Carl: Thanks. I hope it's a girl this time!

폭탄선언을 하다
drop a bombshell
Com/Inf

To suddenly tell someone a shocking/
surprising piece of news
갑자기 누군가에게 충격적인/놀라운 뉴스를 말하다
(비슷한 표현: made one's jaw drop, drop a bomb)

"우리는
캐나다로
이시 갈 거야"

She
dropped
a
bombshell

엄마가 폭탄을 떨어뜨렸어

아내랑 나는 어젯밤 딸에게 **폭탄선언을 했어요.** 우리는 다음
달에 캐나다로 이민 갈 거라고 했죠. 딸은 처음에는 충격받은 것
같았지만, 지금은 신났어요.

* emigrate 이민 가다

**이렇게
말하자:**

칼: 와이프가 어젯밤 나한테 **폭탄선언을 했어.**
루시: 오, 정말? 그게 뭔데?
칼: 또 임신을 했대!
루시: 와! 축하해!
칼: 고마워. 이번엔 딸이면 좋겠어!

037

Eat your words

I went for a job interview last week. My friend Steve said there was no way I would get the job, but I'm going to make him **eat his words**. I have just received an email from the company telling me I've got the job!

Ivan: Robbie said that he's going to beat* me at squash this weekend.

Angela: He is a pretty good player.

Ivan: Yeah, but I've improved a lot. I've been taking squash lessons every day. I'm going to make him **eat his words**!

자기 말이
틀렸음을 인정하다
eat one's words
Com/Inf

To admit that something you said earlier was wrong

이전에 말했던 것이 잘못되었다는 것을 인정하다

네가
한 말을
먹어라

"내가 틀렸어"

전 지난주에 구직 면접을 봤어요. 제 친구 스티브는 제가 그곳에서 일을 구할 방법은 없다고 했지만, 전 **그 말이 틀렸다는 걸 인정하게** 할 거예요. 방금 그 회사에서 제가 합격했다는 이메일을 받았거든요!

이렇게
말하자:

아이븐: 로비는 자기가 이번 주 스쿼시 시합에서 나를 이길 거라고 했어.
안젤라: 로비는 꽤 잘하지.
아이븐: 맞아, 하지만 나 많이 발전했거든. 매일 스쿼시 수업을 받고 있어. 난 **걔 말이 틀렸다는 것을 인정하게** 할 거야!

* beat (게임이나 시합에서) 이기다

038

Egg on your face

I was in the gym with a friend last night. He's a good guy, but he is always talking about how strong he is. He told me he could do 50 push-ups. Then he actually tried to do it. He only did 30. He really had **egg on his face**!

Mavis: My boyfriend saw me yesterday with a guy. He came straight over to me and accused me of* cheating on him!

Tom: Wow, so what happened next?

Mavis: I told him that guy was my cousin. He's visiting from Canada.

Tom: Hahaha! Your boyfriend must have been really embarrassed*. He really had **egg on his face**!

038. MP3

체면을 구김, 망신
egg on one's face
Com/Inf

Extreme embarrassment. Usually the embarrassment is the result of one's own actions.
극도로 당혹스러운. 보통 이러한 당혹스러움은 자기 행동의 결과다.

네 얼굴에 계란

어젯밤에 전 친구와 함께 체육관에 있었어요. 걔는 좋은 녀석이지만 항상 자기가 얼마나 강한지에 대해서 얘기를 해요. 걔는 팔굽혀펴기를 50개 할 수 있다고 했죠. 그러고 나서 실제로 그걸 하려고 했어요. 30개밖에 못 했죠. 걔는 진짜 **체면을 구겼어요**!

이렇게
말하자:

매비스: 내 남자친구가 내가 어떤 남자랑 있는 걸 보고, 곧장 나한테 와서 내가 그 남자랑 바람을 피운다고 비난하는 거야!
톰: 와, 그래서. 다음에 어떻게 됐어?
매비스: 그 남자는 내 사촌이라고 말했지. 사촌이 캐나다에서 왔거든.
톰: 하하하! 네 남친 정말 당황했겠는데. 정말 **체면 구겼네**!

* accuse A of B A를 B 때문에 비난하다/고소하다   * must have p.p. ~했음이 틀림없다(과거 사실에 대한 확신)

039

Feather in your cap

Another feather in your cap

As you go through* life, you learn new skills. It could be learning to play a musical instrument, learning a new computer skill, or learning a language. Whenever you learn a new skill, be proud. It's another feather in your cap.

IN A REAL CONVERSATION

Jeff: How was your driving test yesterday?

Helen: I passed with flying colours*.

Jeff: Excellent! That's another **feather in your cap**!

Helen: Yeah. I'm really happy. I'm going to buy a car next week.

039. MP3

업적, 자랑거리
**feather
in one's cap**
Com/Inf

An achievement to be proud of

Another
feather
in
your
cap

당신 모자에
또 다른 깃털

당신은 인생을 살아가며 새로운 기술을 배웁니다. 악기를
연주하는 것을 배울 수도 있고, 새로운 컴퓨터 기술을 배우거나,
또는 언어를 배우죠. 새 기술을 배울 때마다, 자부심을 가지세요.
그건 또 다른 **자랑거리**입니다.

˙ go through ~을 겪다, ~을 거치다

이렇게
말하자:

제프: 어제 운전면허 시험은 어떻게 됐어?
헬렌: 아주 우수하게 통과했지.
제프: 훌륭해! **자랑거리**가 하나 더 생겼구나!
헬렌: 응, 정말 행복해. 다음 주에 차를 살 거야.

˙ with flying colours 아주 탁월하게(color [AM])

040

Fight fire with fire

Fight fire with fire

When I was in high school, I was frequently picked on by the school bully. So I decided to fight fire with fire! I took Taekwondo lessons for several months. When the bully saw my fighting skills he never bothered me again.

IN A REAL CONVERSATION

Businessperson 1: Our main competitor is advertising right outside our building!

Businessperson 2: Really? Right! It's time to **fight fire with fire**! Let's print off some of our advertising flyers* and hand them out outside their building!

040. MP3

이열치열이다, 맞불을 놓다
fight fire with fire
Com/Inf

To respond to an attack in a similar way
that has been used against you

당신에게 썼던 것과 비슷한 유형의 공격으로 보복하다
이 표현은 19세기에 미국 정착민이 친 더 큰 불에 걸려드
작은 불을 피해 고립됨을 막았던 것에서 유래했다고 한다.

불로 불과 싸워라

저는 고등학교 때 학교 일진에게 자주 괴롭힘을 당했어요.
그래서 **앙갚음하기**로 마음먹었죠! 전 여러 달 동안 태권도
수업을 받았어요. 그 애는 제 싸움 기술을 보더니 다시는 저를
귀찮게 하지 않았어요.

이렇게
말하자:

사업가 1: 우리의 주 경쟁자가 우리 건물 바로 밖에서 광고하고
있어요!

사업가 2: 정말요? 좋아요, **이에는 이, 눈에는 눈, 맞불을 놓을
때입니다!** 우리 광고물을 뽑아서 저쪽 빌딩 밖에서
나눠줍시다!

˙ flyer 광고용 전단지

041

Fire away

I was approached by a student on the street. He was doing an assignment for his school and wanted to know about an expat's* life in Korea. I had some free time, so I told him to fire away with his questions.

IN A REAL CONVERSATION

Dave:	I would like to know more about Korean history. Could I ask you a few questions?
Soyeon:	No problem. **Fire away!**
Dave:	Okay. Why is the name 'Kim' so common in Korea?
Soyeon:	Umm... That's not a history question.

얘기하세요
fire away
Com/Inf

041. MP3

To give someone permission to begin
speaking, especially to ask questions

누군가가 말을 시작하는 것, 특히 질문하는 것을 허락하다

몇 마디
여쭤봐도 될까요?
물론이죠, 쏴보세요!

길에서 한 학생이 나에게 다가왔어요. 그 학생은 학교 과제를
하고 있었고, 한국에 사는 외국인의 삶에 대해 알고 싶어 했어요.
전 좀 시간이 있어서 그에게 **질문을 해**보라고 했죠.

˚ expat 국외 거주자(= expatriate)

· ·

이렇게
말하자:

데이브: 전 한국 역사에 대해 좀 더 알고 싶은데. 제가 몇 가지
　　　　 질문 좀 해도 될까요?
소연:　 그럼요. **물어보세요!**
데이브: 좋아요. 왜 한국에는 김씨가 많죠?
소연:　 음… 그건 역사 문제가 아닌 것 같은데요.

042

Fit like a glove

I bought a new winter jacket this morning. It's not a colour I would usually wear, but the price was very reasonable. It's really warm and it fits like a glove!

IN A REAL CONVERSATION

Carla: Hey Jimmy, your boots are cool! But they look too big for you.

Jimmy: Actually, they **fit like a glove**. I've just got big feet.

Carla: Oh, wow! Yeah, they're like boats!

안성맞춤이다
fit like a glove
Com/Inf

042. MP3

Something (clothing) is the perfect size and shape for someone.

"차려입으세요."
"탈의실"

장갑처럼 딱 맞아!

전 오늘 아침 새 겨울 재킷을 샀어요. 제가 보통 입는 색은 아니지만, 가격이 매우 합리적이었죠. 진짜 따뜻하고 저한테 **안성맞춤이에요!**

이렇게
말하자:

카를라: 이봐 친구, 네 부츠 정말 멋진데! 하지만 너한테 꽤 커 보여.
지미: 실제로는 나한테 **딱이야**. 내 발이 크거든.
카를라: 오, 왜! 응. 그 부츠 항공모함 같아!

043

Fly off the shelves

The new S smartphone is going on sale today. I heard that it's the best smartphone you can buy these days. They are going to fly off the shelves, so I'm going to the shop right now to buy one. I hope I'm not too late!

Shane: There is a new bakery on the high street*. The bread is fantastic. The baker is French and he makes excellent baguettes.

Shannon: Really? I love baguettes. I might go there later and buy some.

Shane: Well, you'd better go soon. I heard that the bread is **flying off the shelves**. There might not be any left if you go too late.

043. MP3

날개 돋친 듯 팔리다,
불티나게 팔리다
fly off the shelves
Com/Inf

To sell very quickly, be very popular

선반으로부터
날아가는

"휴대폰 세일!"

신상 S 스마트폰이 오늘 할인 중이에요. 그게 요즘 살 수 있는 가장 좋은 스마트폰이라고 들었어요. **날개 돋친 듯이 팔리고** 있어서, 지금 당장 상점에 가서 하나 살 거예요. 너무 늦은 건 아니길!

이렇게
말하자:

셰인: 시내에 새로 연 제과점이 있거든. 빵이 진짜 맛있어. 제빵사가 프랑스 사람인데 정말 훌륭한 바게트를 만들어.

셰넌: 정말? 나 바게트 정말 좋아하는데, 나중에 거기 가서 좀 사야겠어.

셰인: 음, 빨리 가는 게 좋을 거야. 빵이 **불티나게 팔린다**고 들었거든. 너무 늦게 가면 남은 게 없을지도 몰라.

˙high street 번화가, 시내 중심가

044

Fob me off

I called my friend to ask him to help me move some furniture, but he said that he was too busy. I think he was just too lazy and was fobbing me off. I bet* he's at home lying on the sofa!

IN A REAL CONVERSATION

Sally:	I'm never going back to that new PC shop again!
David:	Why not?
Sally:	Because I went there to buy a new monitor, and they tried to **fob me off** with a second hand*, low spec monitor at a ridiculous price!

**얼렁뚱땅 넘어가다,
속여 넘기다**

fob someone off

Com/Inf

To persuade someone to accept
something that is of a low quality or
different from what they really want or,
tell someone something that is not true
so that they won't complain

미안…
나 지금
진짜 바빠

날 속이고 있군

전 제 친구에게 가구 좀 옮기는 것을 도와달라고 부탁했어요.
하지만 걔는 너무 바쁘다고 했죠. 하지만 전 그 친구가 그냥
게을러서 **얼렁뚱땅 넘어간다**는 느낌이 들었어요. 걔는 분명히
집에서 소파에 누워 있을 거예요!

˙bet ~을 장담하다

- -

**이렇게
말하자:**

샐리: 난 절대로 그 새 PC 판매점에 다시는 가지 않을 거야!

데이비드: 왜 그러는데?

샐리: 왜냐하면 내가 새 모니터를 사러 갔는데, 그자들이 중고를
가지고 **속여 팔려고** 하는 거야, 낮은 사양의 모니터를 말도
안 되는 가격에!

˙used [AM]

101

My friend is very interested in spiders. She told me that she wants to buy a tarantula. It was funny she should say that, because my other friend is selling a tarantula!

IN A REAL
CONVERSATION

Shirley: I'm going to the airport tomorrow morning. I'm flying to Hong Kong.

Duncan: **Funny you should say that**, my wife's just come back from Hong Kong. She loved it!

Shirley: Oh, really? Maybe she can recommend some good restaurants for me to go to!

045. MP3

마침 얘기를 꺼내니까
하는 말인데
**funny someone
should say that**
Com/Inf

This expression is used when someone says something that you were also thinking about saying or doing. It is also used to refer to a coincidence.

I'm thinking about buying a tarantula!

Funny you should say that!

난 독거미를
살까 생각 중이야!
네가 딱 그걸
말하다니 재밌다!

제 친구는 거미에 관심이 많아요. 걔가 저에게 독거미를 사고 싶다고 말했죠. **마침 걔가 얘기를 꺼내니까 하는 말인데,** 제 다른 친구가 독거미를 팔고 있거든요!

이렇게
말하자:

설리: 난 내일 아침 공항에 가, 홍콩에 가려고.

던컨: **마침 네가 얘기를 꺼내니까 하는 말인데,** 내 아내가 방금 홍콩에서 돌아왔거든. 아내가 정말 그곳을 좋아했어!

설리: 오, 정말? 내가 갈 만한 좋은 식당들을 추천해 줄 수 있겠네!

103

046

Get over it

My girlfriend left me

you'll get over it

My friend has been having a hard time since his girlfriend left him a few weeks ago. They had been together for a few years, so he's feeling really bad. Time is a great healer. He'll **get over it** eventually.

IN A REAL CONVERSATION

Gus: I can't believe Manchester United lost the game last night.

Liane: You'll **get over it**. After all, it's only a game.

Gus: No way! Football is my life!

Liane: I can't understand why people are so crazy about that sport.

극복하다
get over it
Com/Inf

To accept something that happened in the past and move on
과거에 일어났던 것을 받아들이고 앞으로 나아가다

- 여자친구가
  떠났어
- 괜찮아질 거야

제 친구는 몇 주 전 여자친구가 떠난 이후로 힘든 시간을 보내고 있었어요. 그들은 몇 년 동안을 함께 했기 때문에 친구는 정말 기분이 안 좋아요. 시간은 위대한 치유자입니다. 친구도 결국 그것을 **극복할 거**예요.

**이렇게
말하자:**

거스: 지난밤 맨체스터 유나이티드가 시합에 졌다는 것을 믿을 수 없어.

리안: 그냥 **잊어버려**. 결국은, 시합일 뿐이야.

거스: 설마! 축구는 내 인생이야!

리안: 난 왜 사람들이 그렇게 스포츠에 열광하는지 이해가 안 돼.

047

Give you a bell

I haven't heard from my friend Tommy for a while.
He's been backpacking around Europe since he
finished university. I heard that he arrived back last
week. I think I'll **give him a bell**. I bet he's got a lot
of interesting stories to tell!

**IN A REAL
CONVERSATION**

Todd: Can you meet me sometime this week to
discuss a business venture that I think you
might be interested in?

Stacy: Sure, Tod. I'm always looking for new
opportunities. I'll check my schedule and
give you a bell later today.

전화하다
give someone a bell
Brit/Inf

047. MP3

To give someone a call
누군가에게 전화하다
(비슷한 표현: give someone a ring [BR])

I'll give you a bell

너한테
종 하나 줄게

전 제 친구 토미 소식을 한동안 못 들었어요. 토미는 대학을
마친 후 유럽을 돌며 배낭여행을 하고 있었거든요. 전 토미가
지난주에 돌아왔다고 들었어요. **그에게 전화할까** 합니다. 분명
해줄 만한 재미있는 이야기가 많을 거예요!

**이렇게
말하자:**

토드: 네가 솔깃할 만한 투자 사업에 대해 의논하려고 하는데.
이번 주에 언제 한번 볼 수 있어?

스테이시: 당연하지 토드. 난 항상 새로운 기회를 찾고 있어. 내 일정
보고 오늘 늦게 **너한테 전화할게.**

048

Go off the rails

He's going off the rails

During my first year of university, my girlfriend broke up with me. I was really upset and **went off the rails**. I spent a lot of time going to bars and nightclubs rather than studying. I studied much harder in my second year. Now everything is going great!

IN A REAL CONVERSATION

Parent 1: I'm really worried about my son.

Parent 2: Why? What's the problem?

Parent 1: His grades at school are getting worse, and he's hanging out with some bad kids. I think he might have started smoking, too.

Parent 2: Oh dear! It really sounds like he's **going off the rails**!

탈선하다
go off the rails
Con/Inf

048. MP3

To behave in an unacceptable or antisocial way
용납할 수 없거나 반사회적인 방식으로 행동하다

He's going off the rails

쟤가 선로를 벗어나고 있어

대학 1학년 때, 여자친구랑 깨지고, 저는 너무나 화가 나서 **탈선했었어요**. 공부보단 술집과 나이트클럽에서 많은 시간을 보냈죠. 2학년 때는 좀 더 열심히 공부했어요. 지금은 모든 것이 잘되고 있습니다!

이렇게 말하자:

학부모 1: 전 정말 제 아들이 걱정돼요.

학부모 2: 왜요? 문제가 뭔데요?

학부모 1: 학교 성적이 점점 나빠지고 있고 나쁜 애들과 어울려 다니고 있어요. 담배도 피우기 시작한 것 같아요.

학부모 2: 오 이런! 정말 **정도를 벗어나고** 있는 것 같네요!

049

Go on about

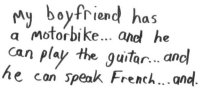

My friend Linda has a new boyfriend. She never stops talking about him and how wonderful he is. She is driving me crazy! I really wish she would stop **going on about** him!

IN A REAL CONVERSATION

Florence:	I saw "BXT" on TV last night. They are so cool! They are so handsome... and they sing and dance so well... and...
Jerry:	(Interrupting) STOP **going on about** K-Pop bands! You talk about them every day! It's driving me crazy!

049. MP3

계속 지껄이다
go on about
Com/Inf

To repeatedly or continuously talk about someone or something, so much so that it annoys other people

계속 반복해서 누군가나 뭔가에 대해 너무 많이 말해서 다른 사람들을 짜증나게 하다

내 남친은 오토바이도 있고, 기타도 다룰 줄 알고, 프랑스어도 할 줄 알고…

개 얘기 좀 그만해!

제 친구 린다에게 새 남자친구가 생겼습니다. 걔는 그 남자가 얼마나 훌륭한지 남자친구에 대해 말하는 것을 절대 멈추지 않아요. 걔 때문에 돌아버리겠어요! 전 진짜 걔가 그 남자**에 대해 계속 지껄이는** 것을 그만 좀 했으면 좋겠어요!

이렇게 말하자:

플로렌스: 나 어젯밤에 TV에서 BXT를 봤어. 걔들은 너무 멋져! 정말 잘 생기고… 그리고 노래와 춤을 정말 잘하고… 그리고…

제리: (끼어들며) 케이팝 밴드 **얘기 좀** 그만해! 넌 매일 걔네 이야기를 하잖아. 정말 날 돌아버리게 만드는구나!

A virus pandemic has been causing problems all over the world in the last few months. A lot of businesses are struggling and the stock market has completely **gone south**. I hope the virus is stopped soon and life can be normal again.

IN A REAL CONVERSATION

Vicky: Hey Tommy, how are your plans going for building a new house?

Tommy: Those plans have **gone south**. The company I paid for all the building materials suddenly disappeared with all my money!

Vicky: Oh, no!

잘못되다,
하락하다, 도망가다
go south
Com/Inf

050. MP3

To become very bad
매우 나빠지다

주식 시장이
남쪽으로 갔어

바이러스 대유행이 지난 몇 달 동안 전 세계적으로 문제를
일으키고 있습니다. 많은 기업이 어려움을 겪고 있으며
주식시장은 완전히 **하락했죠**. 전 바이러스가 곧 끝나고 삶이
다시 정상화될 수 있으면 좋겠어요.

**이렇게
말하자:**

비키: 안녕 토미, 너 새집 짓는 계획은 어떻게 돼 가?

토미: 그 계획은 **망했어**. 내가 건축 자재 대금을 지급한 회사가
내 돈을 몽땅 들고 갑자기 사라졌거든!

비키: 오, 저런!

051

Good to go

You're good to go!

I was stopped by a police officer while driving to work this morning*. It was just a routine check*. I showed him my driving licence and insurance documents. Then I was **good to go**.

Wife:	Are you ready to go to the beach?
Husband:	Almost. I just need to get my towel and suntan lotion. Then I'll be **good to go**!
Wife:	Okay. Don't forget to pack the beach ball!

051. MP3

준비가 된
good to go
Com/Inf

Ready or prepared for something

무언가에 대해 준비나 대비가 되어 있는

(비슷한 표현: ready to go, ready to roll)

가서도
좋습니다!

제가 오늘 아침 운전해서 회사로 출근하는데 경찰이 차를
세웠어요. 그저 일상적인 점검이었죠. 일단 제 운전면허증과
보험 서류들을 보여줬어요. 그때 저는 **준비가 되어** 있었죠.

* while (I was) driving to work this morning
* routine check 정기 검사

**이렇게
말하자:**

아내: 해변에 갈 준비됐어?
남편: 거의 됐어. 수건이랑 썬탠 로션만 챙기면 돼. 그러면 **다 돼!**
아내: 응. 물놀이 공 챙기는 것도 잊지 마!

052

Green fingers

He's got green fingers

My father loves gardening. He spends a lot of time growing* all kinds of flowers, fruit, and vegetables. He's very good at it*. He's got **green fingers**! He also makes money from selling fruit and veg* at the local market.

IN A REAL CONVERSATION

Dave: I love growing plants, especially chillies*, but I'm not very good at it.

Kelly: You should ask Jenny. She's got **green fingers**. She has a lovely big garden. Maybe she can give you some advice.

원예에 능한 사람/재능
green fingers
Com/Inf

052. MP3

If someone has green fingers, they are very skillful at gardening.
누가 초록색 손가락을 가졌다고 하면, 화초 기르는 것에 매우 능숙한 사람이라는 뜻이다.
(비슷한 표현: a green thumb)

초록색 손가락을
가졌어요

He's got green fingers

아버지는 정원 가꾸기를 좋아하세요. 모든 종류의 꽃, 과일과 채소를 기르는 데에 많은 시간을 보냅니다. 그것을 매우 잘하세요. 아버지는 **원예에 능해요!** 아버지는 게다가 지역 시장에서 과일과 채소를 팔아 돈을 버시죠.

*spend ~ time -ing ~하는 데에 ~한 시간을 보내다
*be good at ~하는 데에 능숙하다, ~을 잘하다
*veg = vegetables

이렇게 말하자:

데이브: 난 식물 키우는 걸 정말 좋아해. 특히 고추. 하지만 잘 키우는 건 아니야.

캘리: 제니에게 물어봐. **원예에 소질이 있거든.** 제니는 멋진 커다란 정원을 가지고 있어. 아마 네게 조언을 해 줄 수 있을 거야.

*chilies [AM]

For the last few weeks, I have been trying to find the courage to ask a girl out* on a date. Yesterday I saw her kissing a guy. It was my best friend! I was **green with envy**!

Layla: Congratulations! I heard you got a new job!

Sidney: Yeah, thanks!

Layla: What's wrong? You don't look very happy about it.

Sidney: Well, my older brother has applied for a job at the same company four times, but he was rejected every time. So he's **green with envy** and hasn't spoken to me for over a week.

몹시 질투하는
green with envy
Com/Inf

053. MP3

Very envious
몹시 질투하는 (이 표현은 셰익스피어의 희곡 「오셀로」에서 유래했다. "Beware of jealousy; it is the green-eyed monster which doth mock the meat it feeds on.": 질투를 경계하십시오. 그것은 사람의 마음을 농락하여 먹이로 삼는 녹색 눈의 괴물입니다.)

질투로
파랗게 질린

지난 몇 주 동안, 저는 한 아가씨한테 용기를 내 데이트 신청을 하려고 노력하고 있었어요. 어제 전 그 아가씨가 어떤 남자와 키스하는 것을 봤어요. 바로 제 절친이었죠! 전 **질투가 나 죽을 지경**이에요!

*ask someone out ~에게 데이트 신청하다

이렇게 말하자:

레일라: 축하해, 너 새 직장을 얻었다며!

시드니: 응, 고마워!

레일라: 왜 그래? 너 별로 기쁜 것 같지 않네.

시드니: 음, 우리 형이 같은 회사 일자리에 네 번 지원했는데 전부 거절당했거든. 그래서, 형이 **너무 질투해서** 일주일이 넘게 나하고 말을 안 하고 있어.

Have a hard time

My friend, Sophie, has been **having a hard time** with her boyfriend. I suggested that she break up with him. She did it the very next day! Now that she's single, I think I might ask her for a date!*

Bob: I'm **having a** really **hard time** waking up in the morning. When my phone alarm goes off, I just switch it off and go back to sleep.

Sandy: Why don't you try putting your phone somewhere far from your bed? Then you'll have to get out of your bed to switch it off.

Bob: Yeah, that might work. I'll give it a try!

054. MP3

힘든 시간을 겪다
have a hard time
Com/Inf

To have difficulty with something

뭔가로 어려움을 겪다
[비슷한 표현: Having a rough time]

- 남자친구 때문에
  힘든 시간을 겪고 있어

- 차 버려
- 좋은 생각이야…
  고마워!

제 친구 소피는 남자친구와 **힘든 시간을 겪고** 있어요. 그래서 전
그와 헤어지라고 권했죠. 그녀는 바로 다음 날 그렇게 했어요.
이제 그녀는 싱글이니까, 그녀에게 데이트 신청을 할까 싶어요!

* ask someone for a date ~에게 데이트 신청하다(= ask someone out)

이렇게
말하자:

봅: 아침에 일어나기가 **정말 힘들어**. 휴대폰 알람이 울리면
난 그냥 꺼버리고 다시 잠을 자거든.

샌디: 휴대폰을 침대에서 멀리 떨어진 곳에 두는 건 어때?
그럼 그걸 끄려고 침대에서 일어나야 하니까.

봅: 그래. 그게 먹힐 수도 있겠다. 그렇게 한 번 해볼게.

Have a lie in

Having a lie in ☺

Sunday is my favourite day of the week. I usually work 6 days a week, so I always wake up early except on Sundays. That's the only day I can have a lie in.

Tracey: I'm going to the flea market tomorrow morning to sell some old stuff from my house. Do you want to come?

Tony: No thanks. The flea market starts at 7am. I've had a really busy week, so I'm going to **have a** long **lie in** tomorrow!

늦잠 자다
have a lie in
Brit/Inf

To intentionally stay in bed longer than
you usually would in the morning

침대에 누워 있는

일요일은 제가 가장 좋아하는 요일입니다. 전 평소 주 6일 일하기
때문에 일요일을 제외하고는 항상 일찍 일어납니다. 일요일은
제가 **늦잠을 자는** 유일한 날이에요.

**이렇게
말하자:**

트레이시: 난 내일 아침에 벼룩시장에 가서 우리 집에 있는 낡은
물건들을 좀 팔려고 해. 너도 올래?

토니: 아니 괜찮아. 벼룩시장은 오전 7시에 시작하잖아. 난 정말
바쁜 한 주를 보냈거든. 그래서 난 내일 **늦게까지 푹 잘 거야!**

I like cars. They are very convenient, but I'm not really interested in having a big fancy car. People who buy big fancy cars seem to **have money to burn**. If I were rich, I would just buy a small car and spend more money on other things like travel!

IN A REAL CONVERSATION

Son: Mum*, can you buy me a new computer? I want to play games online, but I need a really good PC.

Mother: What? A new PC just to play games? No way! You should spend more time studying, NOT playing games! Anyway, computers are expensive. We don't **have money to burn**.

돈이 남아돌다
have money to burn
Com/Inf

056. MP3

To have a lot of money to spend on things you don't need

불필요한 것에 많은 돈을 쓰다

태울 돈

전 차를 좋아해요. 차는 매우 편리하지만, 전 크고 화려한 차에는 그다지 관심이 없어요. 크고 화려한 차를 사는 사람들은 **돈이 남아도는** 것처럼 보여요. 만약에 내가 부자라면, 난 그냥 작은 차를 사고 여행 같은 다른 곳에 돈을 더 쓰겠어요!

| 이렇게 말하자: | 아들: | 엄마, 새 컴퓨터 사주시면 안 돼요? 온라인 게임을 하고 싶은데 정말 좋은 PC가 필요하거든요. |
| | 엄마: | 뭐? 단지 게임하려고 새 PC를 사? 말도 안 된다! 넌 게임이 아니라 공부하는데 시간을 더 쏟아야지! 어쨌든, 컴퓨터는 비싸. 우리에게 **남아도는 돈**은 없어. |

* Mom [AM]

Hit the town

Let's hit the town

An old drinking friend of mine has been living and working in America for the last 5 years. He's coming back this weekend for a holiday*. I'm really looking forward to seeing him. We're going to **hit the town** as soon as he arrives!

IN A REAL CONVERSATION

Gemma: I'm so happy! I have finished all my final exams!

Alex: Yeah, me too! Why don't we go out and celebrate?

Gemma: Good idea! I'll go home and change my clothes. Then let's **hit the town**!

나가서 신나게 놀다
hit the town
Com/Inf

057. MP3

To go out (usually at night) and have fun

나가서 (보통, 밤에) 신나게 놀다

시내를 치자

내 오랜 술친구 한 명은 지난 5년간 미국에서 살면서 일하고 있습니다. 이 친구가 이번 주에 휴가 차 돌아와요. 난 정말 이 친구 만나는 걸 기대하고 있어요. 그가 도착하는 대로 우리는 **나가서 신나게 놀** 겁니다!

˙ vacation [AM]

이렇게
말하자:

젬마: 난 정말 행복해! 기말시험이 모두 끝났어!
알렉스: 응, 나도! 우리 축하하러 나갈까?
젬마: 좋은 생각이야! 집에 가서 옷 갈아입고,
나가서 신나게 놀자!

Hold
your
tongue!

I hate bad service in restaurants. Sometimes it's good to complain, but sometimes it's just better to **hold your tongue** and never go back to the restaurant. I complained once while I was on a date. It completely ruined our night.

IN A REAL CONVERSATION

Student: Teacher, I don't want to take the exam this afternoon. I haven't studied. Anyway, exams are stupid! And…

Teacher: **Hold your tongue!** You come to school for education. It's your own fault you didn't study. You WILL take the exam!

058. MP3

입 다물다
hold one's tongue
Com/Inf

To remain silent. To say nothing
침묵하다. 아무 말도 하지 않다

Hold your tongue!

혀를 붙잡아!

난 식당에서 서비스가 형편없는 걸 질색해요. 가끔 항의하는 것도 좋지만, **그냥 잠자코 있다**가 다시는 그 식당에 안 가는 게 나을 때도 있죠. 데이트할 때 한 번 불만을 이야기한 적이 있었는데, 그게 우리의 저녁을 완전히 망쳤거든요!

이렇게
말하자:

학생: 선생님, 저 오늘 오후에 시험 안 보고 싶어요. 공부를 안 했어요. 어쨌든 시험은 바보 같아요. 그리고…

선생님: **조용히 해**! 너는 배우러 학교에 오는 거야. 공부를 안 한 것은 네 잘못이지. 그리고 넌 시험을 보게 될 거야!

059

Housewarming party

Different countries have different kinds of **housewarming party** customs. In the U.K., people often give things like plates or other kitchenware. I was very surprised to learn that Koreans give toilet paper and household cleaning products as housewarming gifts. Actually, those are very practical gifts!

IN A REAL CONVERSATION

Harry: Are you going to Joanne's **housewarming party** tonight?

Jenny: Yes, but I have no idea what kind of gift I should take.

Harry: Well, I know that she loves red wine.

Jenny: Oh, that's easy! I'll buy a nice bottle of French wine and some cheese to go with it!

집들이
housewarming party
Com/Inf

A party to celebrate moving to a new home

새집 이사를 축하하는 파티 ('집을 데운다'라는 표현은 실제로 새집을 데우는 행위에서 나왔다. 아주 옛날 난방장치가 없던 시절에 손님들이 집들이 선물로 장작을 가지고 온 데서 비롯되었다고 한다.)

집 데우는
파티

나라마다 **집들이** 풍습이 달라요. 영국에서는 사람들이 종종 접시나 다른 주방용품 같은 걸 주거든요. 한국인은 집들이 선물로 화장지와 가정용 청소용품을 선물한다는 것을 알고 깜짝 놀랐어요. 사실 뭐, 매우 실용적인 선물이긴 하죠!

이렇게
말하자:

해리: 너 오늘 밤 조안 네 **집들이**에 갈 거야?

제니: 응. 근데 어떤 선물을 골라야 할지 모르겠네.

해리: 글쎄, 조안이 레드와인을 좋아하는 것은 알아.

제니: 아, 그거 좋네! 나는 좋은 프랑스 와인 한 병하고 치즈 좀 사 가야겠다!

060

Hustle and bustle

I spent my childhood in the countryside and moved into the city in my early 20s. At first, I found city life very stressful but I soon got used to the **hustle and bustle**, and now I love it!

Yolanda:	How's your new apartment in Seoul?
Greg:	I love it! Everything is on my doorstep* and a lot of my friends live nearby.
Yolanda:	I'm really happy for you, but doesn't the **hustle and bustle** of the city get stressful sometimes?
Greg:	Sure, so when I get stressed, I go to the countryside for the weekend.

번잡스러움, 북적거림, 혼잡
hustle and bustle
Com/Inf

A lot of noise and activity
(도시의) 소음과 활기

북적이고 서두르고

전 어린 시절을 시골에서 보내고 이십 대 초반에 도시로 이사를 했어요. 처음에는 도시 생활이 너무 스트레스라는 것을 알게 되었지만, 곧 **북적임**에 익숙해졌고, 지금은 그것이 정말 좋아요!

이렇게 말하자:

율란다: 서울의 새 아파트는 어때?

그렉: 정말 좋아! 모든 것이 바로 집 앞에 있고, 많은 친구가 근처에 살아.

율란다: 네가 좋아하니 나도 정말 기쁘긴 한데, **혼잡한** 도시가 때로는 스트레스가 되지 않아?

그렉: 맞아, 그래서 스트레스받을 때면, 난 주말에 시골로 가.

* on my doorstep 집 앞에, 아주 가까운 곳에(= very close by)

I could eat a horse

I am absolutely starving! I haven't eaten breakfast or lunch. I'm really looking forward to having a huge, delicious dinner. I'm so hungry I could eat a horse! Maybe I'll have Korean barbecue!

Jane: Hey Denver, I'm going to the steak restaurant on Main Street tonight. Do you want to come?

Denver: Definitely! I'm so hungry **I could eat a horse**, and I LOVE that restaurant!

Jane: Okay! Let's meet there at 7pm.

배가 너무 고프다
I could eat a horse
Com/Inf

I am very hungry.

너무 배고파서
말 한 마리도
먹을 수 있겠어!

I'm so hungry I could eat a horse!

배고파 죽겠어요! 전 아침도 점심도 먹지 못했어요. 전 푸짐하고 맛있는 저녁을 정말 기대하고 있어요. 너무 배고파서 **말 한 마리도 먹을 수 있을 것 같아요!** 아마 전 삼겹살을 먹을 거예요!

이렇게
말하자:

제인: 있잖아, 덴버, 오늘 밤 메인 가에 있는 스테이크 식당에 갈 건데 너도 올래?

덴버: 당연하지! 배가 너무 고파서 **말 한 마리도 다 먹을 수 있을 것 같아.** 그리고 난 그 식당 정말 좋아해.

제인: 좋아! 7시에 거기에서 보자.

062

In one ear and out the other

Having kids can be difficult. Living with teenagers can be hard work. They have so many things going on in their lives that they can be difficult to talk to.* Sometimes it seems that what you say to them just goes **in one ear and out the other**!

Wife:	Did you buy milk on your way home?
Husband:	Huh? What are you talking about?
Wife:	I asked you this morning to buy some milk on your way home from work.
Husband:	Sorry, I don't remember you asking me.
Wife:	Wow, sometimes when I talk to you, it just goes **in one ear and out the other**!

한 귀로 듣고
한 귀로 흘려서
**in one ear and
out the other**
Com/Inf

062. MP3

Heard, but ignored, disregarded, or
swiftly forgotten
한 귀 귀었다가 다그쳐가나 깨러 잊여버리다

"한 귀로 듣고
한 귀로 흘리고"

너 숙제해야지!

아이를 키우는 건 힘들 수 있습니다. 십대와 사는 건 어려운
일이죠. 그 애들의 삶에서 너무 많은 일들이 일어나서 대화가
안 돼요. 가끔 그 애들은 당신의 말을 그냥 **한 귀로 듣고 한 귀로
흘리는** 것처럼 보여요.

° so ~ that … 너무나 ~해서 …하다

이렇게
말하자:

아내: 당신 집에 오는 길에 우유 사 왔어?
남편: 어? 무슨 소리야?
아내: 내가 오늘 아침에, 당신 퇴근길에 우유 좀 사달라고
부탁했는데.
남편: 미안, 당신이 부탁한 걸 잊어버렸어.
아내: 와, 가끔, 당신은 내가 얘기할 때 그냥 **한 귀로 듣고 한 귀로
흘려** 버린다니까!

063

In her pocket

She's got him in her pocket

My friend adores his girlfriend. He thinks she's the best. He does everything for her. The problem is, she takes advantage of* him. She makes him do EVERYTHING for her. She's got him in her pocket.

Police officer 1: The crime in this city has increased SO much this year! What's going on?

Police officer 2: It's the mafia. They are paying huge bribes. They have the politicians **in their pocket**.

063. MP3

통제 하에 있는,
손아귀에 쥐고 흔드는
in one's pocket
Com/Inf

Negatively controlled or influenced by someone. If you have someone in your pocket, they are in your control.

저 여자는
그를 주머니에
넣고 다녀

She's got him in her pocket

내 친구는 자기 여자친구를 무척 사랑해요. 그녀가 최고라고 생각하죠. 그녀를 위해 무엇이든 합니다. 문제는, 그녀가 그를 이용한다는 거예요. 자기를 위해 모든 것을 하게 만들어요. 그 여자는 내 친구를 **손아귀에 쥐고 흔들어요.**

take advantage of ~을 이용하다

이렇게
말하자:

경찰 1: 올해, 이 도시에서 범죄가 너무 많이 증가했어요! 무슨 일일까요?

경찰 2: 마피아예요. 그들이 막대한 뇌물을 주고 있어요. 정치인들을 **자기들 통제하에 두고** 있죠.

064

In the mood for

The weather is fantastic today! It's so sunny! Summer weather always puts me **in the mood for** swimming and sunbathing. I think I'll go to the beach!

Wife:	Let's go out for dinner tonight.
Husband:	Good idea! What do you feel like eating?
Wife:	I'm **in the mood for** something spicy.
Husband:	How about Indian curry? There's a good Indian restaurant in town.
Wife:	Perfect! Let's go there.

064. MP3

하고 싶어서, 기분이 나서
in the mood for
Com/Inf

Desiring having or doing something

"나는 이런 걸 할 기분이야"

I'M IN THE MOOD FOR...

해변에서 쉴
나이트클럽에서 춤을 출

오늘 날씨가 끝내 주네요! 정말 화창해요! 여름 날씨는 늘 수영이나 일광욕을 **하고 싶게** 해요. 난 해변으로 가야겠어요!

이렇게
말하자:

아내: 오늘 저녁엔 나가서 먹자.
남편: 좋은 생각이야! 뭘 먹고 싶어?
아내: 난 뭔가 매운 것이 **당기는데.**
남편: 인도 카레는 어때? 시내에 괜찮은 인도 식당이 있거든.
아내: 정말 좋아! 거기로 가자.

065

In your dreams

My sister wants to be a Hollywood star. I think that will be impossible. She has absolutely no acting experience, and it's a very competitive industry, so I told her, "In your dreams!"

Dan: I hate working in an office. I've decided that I'm going to be a professional athlete!

Linda: Ha! **In your dreams!** You're 45 years old. You're too old to start training. There are SO many people who spend their whole lives trying to become famous athletes, but they don't succeed.

065. MP3

꿈 같은 얘기야
in your dreams
Com/Inf

This expression is used to say that something strongly desired (by another person) will never happen.

난 할리우드
스타가 될 거야!

꿈에서!

내 여동생은 할리우드 스타가 되고 싶어 합니다. 제 생각엔, 그건 불가능할 것 같아요. 그 애는 연기 경험이 전혀 없고, 경쟁이 치열한 분야라서, 전 동생에게 **"꿈같은 얘기야!"**라고 말했어요.

이렇게
말하자:

댄: 난 사무실에서 일하는 게 싫어. 난 프로 운동선수가 되기로 결심했어!

린다: 해! **어림없는 소리 마**! 넌 마흔다섯 살이야. 훈련을 시작하기엔 너무 늙었다고. 유명한 운동선수가 되려고 평생을 바치는 사람이 너무 많은데, 그런 사람도 성공하지 못 해.

I asked my boss today if there was any chance
I could go home early. He told me that there was
no chance because there was too much work to
be completed. I had free movie tickets for tonight,
but I had to give them away to a friend!

IN A REAL CONVERSATION	Tommy:	Hana, **is there any chance** I could borrow some money for lunch? I left my wallet at home.
	Hana:	How much do you need?
	Tommy:	Ummm, 10 pounds?
	Hana:	No problem! Here you are. Pay me back anytime!

066. MP3

…할 가능성이 있을까?
Is there any chance ...?
Com/Inf

This expression is used when asking if it is possible for someone to do something for you.

제가 오늘 일찍
집에 갈 가능성이
있을까요?

없어

전 오늘 사장님께 집에 일찍 갈 **수 있을지** 여쭤봤어요. 사장님은 저에게 끝낼 일이 너무 많아서 그럴 가능성은 없다고 했죠. 전 오늘 공짜 영화표가 있었지만, 그걸 친구한테 줘야만 했어요!

이렇게
말하자:

토미: 하나, 나 점심 먹게 돈 좀 빌려줄 **수 있어**? 지갑을 집에 두고 왔거든.

하나: 얼마가 필요한데?

토미: 음, 10파운드?

하나: 그래! 여기 있어. 아무 때나 갚아!

It takes two to tango

One of my friends told me that I argue with him too much. That doesn't make sense* to me. A person can't argue alone. After all, it takes two to tango!

Businessperson 1: So, I would like you to tell me how we are going to sort out* this disagreement about the contract.

Businessperson 2: Well, I think it would be better if we schedule a formal meeting to discuss this. After all, **it takes two to tango**.

067. MP3

손바닥도 마주쳐야
소리가 난다
It takes two to tango
Com/Inf

This expression is used when
emphasizing that both people/parties in
a difficult situation must accept blame.

탱고 추려면
두 명이
필요해

내 친구 하나가 그러는데 내가 자기랑 너무 많이 다툰다는
거예요. 하지만 난 이해가 가지 않아요. 사람이 혼자서 다툴 수는
없잖아요. 결국 **손바닥도 마주쳐야 소리가 난다**고요!

˙ make sense 이해가 되다, 타당하다

....

이렇게
말하자:

사업가 1: 그럼, 전 우리가 이 계약에 대한 의견 차이를 어떻게 처리할
것인지 말씀해 주시면 좋겠어요.

사업가 2: 음, 전 우리가 이 문제를 논의하기 위해 공식적인 회의
일정을 잡는 편이 좋을 것 같습니다. 결국 **손바닥도
마주쳐야 소리가 나니**까요.

˙ sort out (문제를) 해결하다, 분류하다

It's written all over your face

A detective was interrogating* a suspect about a crime. The suspect repeatedly claimed his innocence, but the suspect's body language and facial expressions made him appear guilty. It was written all over his face!

IN A REAL CONVERSATION

(Ellen has a big smile on her face)

Jerry: You got the scholarship?

Ellen: No way! How did you know?

Jerry: Because **it's written all over your face!** Congratulations!

Ellen: Thank you!

068. MP3

얼굴에 다 써 있다
It's written all over one's face
Com/Inf

Everyone can tell how you are feeling just by looking at your face.

네 얼굴에
다 써 있어!

"내가 했음/범인은
바로 나/유죄"

한 형사가 용의자를 범죄 혐의로 심문하고 있었어요. 용의자는 거듭 자신의 결백을 주장했지만, 그의 몸짓과 표정에서 유죄라는 게 보였죠. **그의 얼굴에 그렇게 쓰여 있었어요!**

ˈinterrogate 심문하다. 질문하다, 정보를 얻다

이렇게
말하자:

(엘렌이 얼굴에 함박웃음을 짓고 있다)

제리: 너 장학금 받았구나?

엘렌: 말도 안 돼! 너 어떻게 알았어?

제리: **네 얼굴에 그렇게 쓰여 있으니까!** 축하해!

엘렌: 고마워!

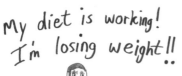

I've been on a diet* for a few months now. I've lost 10 kilos. It's been hard work, because I've stopped eating a lot of my favourite* foods, but I'm determined to **keep it up** because I feel much healthier now!

Husband: Well, darling, I've been studying Korean for a year now, and now I can make conversation with* the staff in the local Korean restaurant!

Wife: Wow! Good job! **Keep it up**! You're going to be my own personal interpreter when we go on holiday to Korea this summer!

069. MP3

계속해 나가다, 힘내다
keep it up
Com/Inf

To continue doing something. We can use this expression to encourage someone to continue doing something well.

뭔가를 계속하다. 누군가에게 계속 뭔가를 잘하라고 격려할 때에도 이 표현을 사용할 수 있다.

다이어트가
효과가 있어!
살이 빠지고
있다고!

잘했어! 계속
그렇게 해!

난 지금 몇 달째 다이어트 중이에요. 10킬로 뺐죠. 내가 좋아하는 음식을 많이 먹지 않아서 힘들었지만, 난 지금 훨씬 건강해진 것 같아서 **계속하기**로 결심했어요.

*be on a diet 다이어트(식이요법) 중이다
*favorite [AM]

- -

**이렇게
말하자:**

남편: 음, 자기야, 난 지금 1년째 한국어 공부를 하고 있는데. 이제 현지 한식당 직원들과 대화도 나눌 수 있어!

아내: 왜 잘했네 **힘내**! 우리 이번 여름에 한국으로 휴가 갈 때 당신이 내 개인 통역사 하면 되겠어!

*make conversation with ~와 대화하다

Living in a big city can be very expensive. First of all, apartment rent is very high. I also work long hours, so I spend quite a lot of money eating in restaurants because I don't have enough time to cook. I have a reasonable income though, so I manage to* **keep the wolf from the door**.

IN A REAL CONVERSATION

Jane: Hey Andy! How's it going? The last time we spoke, you were worried about money. Are things okay now?

Andy: Yeah, I asked my boss if I could work some overtime to make some extra money. I'm working an extra hour every day, so now I'm managing to **keep the wolf from the door**!

입에 풀칠은 하다
**keep the wolf
from the door**
Com/Inf

To have just enough money to be able to pay for life's essentials like food and housing
음식이나 집 같은 생활필수품을 위한 충분한 돈을 갖다
(이 표현에서 문 앞의 늑대는 가족에 대한 위험이나 고난을 나타낸다. '늑대를 문에서 멀리 둔다'라는 것은 당신이 가족을 보호한다는 뜻이다)

늑대를
문에서
멀리 둬

대도시에 산다는 것은 비용이 많이 들 수 있어요. 일단 아파트 임대료가 매우 높아요. 게다가 전 장시간 일하기 때문에 요리할 시간이 충분치 않아 외식으로 꽤 많은 돈을 써요. 하지만 전 적당한 수입이 있어서, 그럭저럭 **입에 풀칠은 하죠**.

*manage to 간신히 ~하다, 어떻게든 ~해내다

**이렇게
말하자:**

제인: 앤디! 요즘 어떻게 지내? 지난번에 얘기할 때, 너 돈 걱정을 했잖아. 이제 괜찮아?

앤디: 응, 내가 상사에게 여윳돈을 벌기 위해 야근을 할 수 있는지 물어봤어. 난 매일 한 시간씩 초과 근무를 하고 있어서 간신히 **입에 풀칠은 하고 있어!**

071 Keep your cards close to your chest

keep your
cards
close to
your
chest

I have an exciting new idea to improve my business, but I'm going to **keep my cards close to my chest**. If another competing business finds out about my idea, they might use it.

Husband:	I think I'm going to quit my job next month. I've been offered a better job with another company.
Wife:	Well, **keep your cards close to your chest** until you've made a firm decision. If the boss finds out that you're thinking about quitting, he might fire you.

생각을 숨기다,
은밀히 행하다
**keep one's cards
close to one's
chest**
Com/Inf

071. MP3

To keep one's planned actions secret
계획된 행동을 비밀로 유지하다 (이 표현은 카드 게임을 할
때 카드를 가슴 가까이에 바짝 붙여서 상대방이 못 보게 하
는 것에서 유래했다)

패를 가슴에
가깝게 대다

keep your
cards
close to
your
chest

제 사업을 발전시킬 만한 흥미로운 아이디어가 있습니다만, 전
제 **생각을 숨기려고** 합니다. 만에 하나 경쟁사가 제 아이디어를
알게 되면 그들이 그것을 사용할지 모르니까요.

**이렇게
말하자:**

남편: 나 다음 달에 일을 그만둘까 해. 다른 회사에서 더 나은
일자리를 제안받았거든.

아내: 음. 결정을 확실히 내릴 때까지 **은밀하게 해**. 사장님이 당신이
그만둘 생각을 하고 있다는 걸 알면 당신을 해고할 수도 있어.

072

Keep your hair on

A car drove through a puddle and splashed dirty water all over me! I was so angry and shouted at the driver. As he drove away, he just laughed and shouted back at me, "**Keep your hair on!**" That made me even angrier!

IN A REAL CONVERSATION

Kelvin: I just got my mock school test results back, and I failed everything! I can't believe it! I'm so stressed. What am I going to do?

Clare: **Keep your hair on!** It's not a big deal.* They're only mock tests. They're not that important. Your results are usually good. You have plenty of time to study before the real tests.

열 내지 마라,
열 올리지 마라, 진정해라
keep one's hair on
Brit/Inf

Don't get angry. Stay calm. Don't lose your temper.

화내지 마, 진정해. 열 올리지 마. (이 표현은 1800년대 중반으로 거슬러 올라간다. 당시 영국 상류층 남성들은 가발을 썼는데, 화가 나면 가발을 벗어 땅에 내동댕이쳤다고 한다) (비슷한 표현: keep your shirt on [AM])

가발은 쓰고 있어!

어떤 차가 웅덩이를 지나가면서 나한테 온통 더러운 물을 튀겼어요! 난 너무 화가 나서 운전자에게 소리를 질렀죠. 그 사람은 차를 몰고 가면서, 그냥 웃으면서 제게 **"열 올리지 말라고!"**라고 소리치더군요. 그게 저를 더욱 화나게 했어요!

이렇게 말하자:	
켈빈:	난 방금 학교 모의고사 결과를 받았는데, 모두 망쳤어! 믿을 수가 없어! 나 너무 스트레스받아. 어떡하지?
클레어:	**침착해**! 별거 아니야, 그냥 모의시험일 뿐이야. 그렇게 중요하지 않아. 네 결과는 그런대로 괜찮잖아. 실제 시험 전에 공부할 시간은 충분해.

*It's not a big deal. 큰 문제가 아니야, 걱정 마 (= It's not a big problem. Don't worry about it.)

073

Keep your head above water

Keep your head above water

I was quite poor when I attended university, but I always managed to find part-time jobs. The money I earned helped me to **keep my head above water**. And I also got a lot of work experience.

IN A REAL CONVERSATION

Jill: How's your study going for your Master's degree?

Bob: Well, my professor has given me a lot of research to do, but it's going okay. I'm **keeping my head above water**.

Jill: Keep it up. You can do it!

073. MP3

간신히 꾸려 나가다
keep one's head above water
Com/Inf

To manage to survive, especially financially, or to keep up with some difficult work or task

그럭저럭 살아 나가다, 특히 재정적으로, 혹은 어려운 일이나 임무를 해내다

내 머리를
수면 위에
유지해

전 대학에 다닐 때 무척 가난했지만, 항상 아르바이트를 찾아다녔고, 제가 번 돈으로 혼자 **간신히 꾸려 나갈** 수 있었죠. 게다가 많은 업무 경험을 쌓았어요.

이렇게 말하자:

질: 석사 학위 준비는 잘 되고 있어?

봅: 음, 우리 교수님이 나한테 연구 조사할 것을 많이 주셨지만, 괜찮을 거야. **간신히 하고 있어.**

질: 기운 내. 넌 할 수 있어!

074

Kill time

When you're waiting for someone or something, or you just have some free time on your hands, what do you do to **kill time**? Personally, I like to watch funny videos on the internet, and if I have a lot of time to kill, I love to cook!

IN A REAL CONVERSATION

Janet: Why are you drinking beer in a bar in the afternoon?

Sam: My wife is shopping for clothes. I hate clothes shopping, so I'm just **killing time** until she finishes.

Janet: Ah, I see. I'm meeting my friend here for lunch. I've heard the food is great here!

시간을 때우다
kill time
Com/Inf

To do something to occupy time while you are waiting for something else to happen

다른 일을 기다리는 동안에 시간을 때우기 위해서 무언가를 하다

시간 죽이기

여러분이 누군가를 또는 뭔가를 기다릴 때, 또는 자유시간이 생겼을 때, 뭘 하면서 **시간을 때우나요**? 개인적으로, 전 인터넷에서 재미있는 영상을 보는 것을 좋아하고, 만약 시간이 많다면 요리하는 것을 진짜 좋아해요!

이렇게 말하자:

자넷: 왜 오후에 바에서 맥주를 마시고 있는 거야?

샘: 아내가 옷을 사고 있어. 난 옷 쇼핑을 싫어해서, 마칠 때까지 **시간을 죽이고** 있는 거야.

자넷: 아, 그래. 난 여기서 친구 만나서 점심 먹을 거야. 여기 음식이 훌륭하다고 들었거든!

I was at my friend's house, and I noticed that she had a very nice, expensive bottle of wine. I asked my friend if I could have some. She told me, "**Knock yourself out**!" So I did. Actually, it was so good that I drank the whole bottle. My friend has never invited me back to her house.

IN A REAL CONVERSATION

Sandy: Hey Milo! That's a really cool drone you've got! Do you mind if* I borrow it for a couple of hours and take it down to* the park?

Milo: Sure, **knock yourself out**. I'm not planning to use it today.

마음대로 해라
knock oneself out
Com/Inf

075. MP3

Go ahead. Do as one pleases. Give
permission/approval (often when the
speaker is not interested in the outcome)
계속하다. 마음대로 하다. 허락/승인하다 (종종, 말하는 사
람이 결과에 관심이 없을 때)

네 자신을
때려!

친구 집에 갔었는데, 아주 괜찮은, 비싼 와인이 있는 것을
눈치챘어요. 친구한테 내가 좀 마셔도 되는지 물어봤죠. 친구는
"마음대로 해"라고 했어요! 그래서 그렇게 했죠. 사실 너무
맛있어서 한 병을 다 비웠어요. 그 친구는 다시는 저를 집에
부르지 않았어요.

**이렇게
말하자:**

샌디: 이봐 마일로! 네가 가지고 있는 드론 정말 멋지다!
내가 두어 시간만 빌려서 공원으로 가져가도 될까?

마일로: 물론이지. **마음대로 해.** 오늘은 그거 사용할 계획이 없어.

*Do you mind if ~해도 되겠습니까?   *take down to ~로 이동시키다

076

Let it go

My friend, Jack, has recently been dumped by his girlfriend. Every time I meet him, he complains about it* and sometimes he even starts to cry. I tell him over and over that he needs to just **let it go**!

IN A REAL CONVERSATION

Luke: I can't believe it. I lost my life savings on the stock market!

Anna: Luke, you took a gamble and you made a mistake. Everyone makes mistakes.

Luke: But I lost SO much money!

Anna: Stop! You still have a good job and you have your health. Money comes and goes. You need to just **let it go**.

076. MP3

내버려 두다, 그쯤 해두다
let it go
Com/Inf

To stop stressing, thinking or being angry about something that happened in the past

과거에 있어났던 일에 대해 스트레스를 받거나 생각하거나 학내는 것을 멈추다

그냥 그게
가도록
내버려 둬

제 친구 잭은 최근에 여자친구에게 차였어요. 만날 때마다 그 친구는 차인 것에 대해 넋두리를 늘어놓고 가끔 울기까지 해요. 전 그에게 그냥 **그쯤 해두**라고 계속 말하죠!

° it = he has recently been dumped by his girlfriend

이렇게
말하자:

루크: 믿을 수가 없어. 평생 저축한 재산을 주식으로 날렸어!
안나: 루크, 넌 투자했고 실수를 한 거야. 누구나 실수는 해.
루크: 하지만 난 너무 많은 돈을 잃었다구!
안나: 그맨 넌 여전히 좋은 직장이 있고 건강해. 돈은 돌고 도는 거야. 그냥 **내버려 둬**.

077

Like bees to honey

Whenever a new smartphone comes on the market, consumers are **like bees to honey**. Everyone wants to be the first to own the latest model. I can't believe that some people even start queueing the night before!

Jake: I picked up my new motorbike from the bike shop!

Eva: Oh yeah? Are you happy with it?

Jake: Yeah! It's fantastic! When I parked it in the high street, everyone was impressed and came over to see it. They were **like bees to honey**!

벌떼같이 모인
like bees to honey
Com/Inf

Large numbers of people are attracted to something.

많은 사람이 무언가에 끌리다.

벌이 꿀로
가는 것처럼

Like bees to honey

HONEY

시중에 새 스마트폰이 출시될 때마다 소비자들은 **벌떼같이 모여**듭니다. 모두가 최신 모델을 소유하는 첫 번째 사람이 되기를 원하죠. 심지어 어떤 사람들은 전날 밤부터 줄 서기 시작한다는 게 믿기지 않아요!

이렇게 말하자:

제이크: 나 오토바이 매장에서 새로 산 오토바이 가져왔어!
이바: 오 그래? 마음에 들어?
제이크: 응! 끝내줘! 내가 번화가에 주차했을 때, 다들 감격해서 오토바이를 보러 왔어. **벌떼같이 모여**들었지!

078

Like there's no tomorrow

I met a friend in the pub last night. He recently lost his job, so he was quite depressed and was drinking **like there was no tomorrow**. I tried to cheer him up, but he was so drunk and tired that he fell asleep.

....

IN A REAL CONVERSATION

Erica: I saw your wife in the department store yesterday. She had loads of* shopping bags!

Rob: Yeah, I got a promotion and a pay rise last week. Since then, she's been spending money **like there's no tomorrow**!

Erica: Oh, that explains it! I thought maybe she had won the lottery!

078. MP3

내일이 없는 듯이
like there's no tomorrow
Com/Inf

(Do something) Very quickly and without much thought of the consequences

결과에 대해서 별생각 없이 뭔가를 아주 빠르게 (해치워 버리다)

"내일이
없는 것처럼"
술을 마시고 있어

지난밤 술집에서 한 친구를 만났어요. 그는 최근에 실직해서 아주 우울해했고, **마치 내일 따위는 없다는 듯이** 술을 마시고 있었죠. 저는 그를 격려하고 싶었지만, 그는 너무 취한 데다 피곤해서 잠이 들었어요.

**이렇게
말하자:**

에리카: 나 어제 백화점에서 네 와이프를 봤어. 쇼핑백을 잔뜩 들고 있던데!

롭: 응, 나 지난주에 승진해서 월급이 인상됐어. 그때부터 와이프는 **앞으로 어떻게 되든 말든** 돈을 쓰고 있어!

에리카: 오, 이제 이해가 가네. 난 네 와이프가 복권에라도 당첨된 줄 알았어!

* loads of 수많은

169

079

Light-fingered

There is a guy who lives in my neighbourhood called Larry. He's a professional shoplifter*, but he's been caught many times. Everyone calls him **light-fingered** Larry.

Mia: Have you met the guy who has just moved into the apartment next to me?

Tom: No, but I've heard rumours* about him. Don't ever let him into your home. I heard that he's **light-fingered** and will steal anything.

Mia: Oh, that's a shame. He's really handsome. I was hoping to meet him!

079. MP3

손버릇이 나쁜, 도벽이 있는
light-fingered
Com/Inf

This expression describes someone who has a habit of stealing things.
도벽을 가진 사람을 나타내는 표현이다.

저 자는
손가락이
가벼워!

"좀도둑은 고발함"

우리 동네에 래리라는 남자가 살아요. 그 남자는 도둑질로 먹고 사는 사람인데 여러 번 붙잡혔죠. 모두 그 남자를 '**손버릇 나쁜** 래리'라고 부릅니다.

* shoplifter (가게 등의) 좀도둑

이렇게
말하자:

미아: 너 우리 옆집으로 막 이사 온 남자 본 적 있어?

톰: 아니, 하지만 그 사람에 대한 소문은 들었어. 절대 너희 집에 들이지 마. 그 사람 **도벽이 있어서** 뭐든 훔칠 거라고 하더라고.

미아: 오, 그것참 아깝다. 그 사람 진짜 잘 생겼던데. 그 사람하고 잘되길 바라고 있었거든!

* rumors [AM]

080

Lighten up

My work colleague is having a hard time with the piles of work he has to do. He's getting really stressed and losing sleep over it. If he doesn't **lighten up**, he's going to have a nervous breakdown.

IN A REAL CONVERSATION

Monica: Aaargh! My kids keep asking me to take them to the movies, but I've been working hard and I'm totally exhausted.

Bob: Wow! You need to **lighten up**. You shouldn't be getting this stressed. Actually, I can help you out. I'll take your kids to the movie theatre*. You stay home and get some rest.

080. MP3

기운 내다, 긴장을 풀다
lighten up
Com/Inf

To become less serious and relax more
덜 진지하고 더 느긋해지다 (비슷한 표현: chill out)

너는 마음을
가볍게 할
필요가 있어

저의 직장 동료는 할 일이 산더미처럼 쌓여서 힘들어해요.
그 사람은 점점 더 스트레스를 받아 잠을 못 자고 있어요.
그가 **기운을 차리지** 않는다면, 그는 신경쇠약에 걸릴 거예요.

이렇게
말하자:

모니카: 아아악! 우리 애들이 계속 극장에 데려가 달라고 조르고
있는데, 난 너무 힘들게 일해서 완전히 지쳤다고.

밥: 왜! 좀 **진정해**. 넌 이런 것에 스트레스를 받으면 안 돼. 사실,
내가 도와줄 수 있어. 내가 너희 애들을 영화관에 데리고 갈게.
넌 집에서 좀 쉬어.

* theater [AM]

081

Look before you leap

I was on holiday in Australia a few months ago.
My friends and I rented a small boat and took it out
to sea. I was just about to* dive into the water for
a swim. Luckily, I looked into the water first. There
was a shark right next to the boat! It's always better
to **look before you leap**.

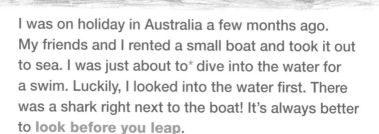

IN A REAL CONVERSATION

Ella: I can't believe it! I just bought stocks for the first time, I lost 5,000 pounds in just 2 hours!

Tom: Wow, I've never bought stocks. If I ever do, I'll research very carefully first. You really need to **look before you leap** when you invest in stocks.

081. MP3

돌다리도
두드려보고 건너라
**look before
you leap**
Com/Inf

To think carefully before taking action.
To consider possible negative outcomes
잘 생각해 보고 행동하다. 부정적인 결과의 가능성을 고려
하다 (비슷한 표현: think before you act)

뛰기 전에
살펴봐

전 몇 달 전 호주에서 휴가를 보내고 있었어요. 친구들과
저는 작은 보트를 빌려서 바다에 나갔어요. 저는 막 수영을
하러 물속으로 뛰어들 참이었죠. 다행히 전 먼저 물속을
들여다봤어요. 보트 바로 옆에 상어가 있는 거예요! 항상
돌다리도 두드려 보고 건너는 것이 좋죠.

* **be about to** 막 ~하려고 하다

이렇게
말하자:

엘라: 믿을 수가 없어! 방금 난생처음 주식을 샀는데, 단 두 시간
만에 5,000파운드를 잃었어!

톰: 와, 난 생전 주식을 사 본 적이 없어. 만약에 산다면, 나는 먼저
아주 신중하게 조사를 할 거야. 주식 투자를 할 때 너 정말
잘 생각해 보고 행동할 필요가 있어.

082

Loose lips sink ships

People who work in the armed forces really do need to be careful talking about military movements and activities. If a spy were to overhear* this kind of information, it could be used by the enemy in war. **Loose lips** really can **sink ships**!

IN A REAL CONVERSATION

Businessperson 1: It's incredible! We've developed a new technology that is going to make us SO rich and famous!

Businessperson 2: Yes, but please be careful. Don't talk to ANYONE about this. You know what they say, **loose lips sink ships**.

입이 가벼우면 화를 부른다
loose lips
sink ships
Com/Inf

Saying too much or releasing confidential information can have dangerous results.
말이 너무 많거나 비밀 정보를 공개하는 것은 위험한 결과를 초래할 수 있다. (이 표현은 제2차 세계대전 중 군사 활동에 관해 공개적으로 말해서는 안 된다는 것을 알리기 위한 선전 포스터에서 유래했다.)

쉿! 헐거운 입술은
배를 가라앉게
한다고

군대에서 일하는 사람들은 군사적인 움직임이나 활동에 관해 말할 때 정말로 신중히 처리해야 합니다. 만약 스파이가 이런 종류의 정보를 우연히 엿듣는다면, 그건 전쟁에서 적에게 이용될 수 있죠. **입이 가벼우면** 정말 **화를 부를** 수 있어요!

˚ overhear 우연히 엿듣다

이렇게
말하자:

사업가 1: 믿을 수 없어! 우리는 우리를 엄청 부유하고 유명하게 만들어 줄 새로운 기술을 개발했어요!

사업가 2: 네, 하지만 조심하세요. 이 일에 대해 누구에게도 말하지 마세요. **입이 가벼우면 화를 부른다**는 말이 있죠.

083

Make my day

It was my wife's birthday yesterday. I bought her some new clothes and took her out for a nice meal. When we got home, I gave her a bottle of her favourite champagne. That really made her day!

IN A REAL
CONVERSATION

Tommy:	I have worked SO hard during my first year in my current job. This morning, my boss gave me a promotion and a pay increase!
Lucy:	That's excellent! You must be over the moon.*
Tommy:	Yeah, it truly **made my day**.

083. MP3

행복하게 하다
make one's day
Com/Inf

To make you feel very happy

생일 축하해!
와! 샴페인 너무
좋아! 고마워!
당신이 나의 하루로
만들어줬어

어제는 아내의 생일이었어요. 전 새 옷을 좀 사주고 근사한
식사를 하려고 아내를 데리고 나갔죠. 우리가 집에 왔을 때,
전 아내가 가장 좋아하는 샴페인 한 병을 줬어요. 아내의 하루를
정말 최고로 **행복하게 해**주었어요!

이렇게
말하자:

토미: 나는 지금 직장에서 첫 한 해 동안 아주 열심히 일해왔어.
오늘 아침 사장님이 날 승진시키고 임금 인상을 해주셨어!

루시: 정말 잘됐다! 너 정말 기쁘겠다!

토미: 응. 정말 덕분에 **하루가 행복해졌지.**

* over the moon 하늘을 둥둥 떠다니는 듯한. 너무나도 황홀한(= very happy)

179

084

Mumbo jumbo

I had a long meeting with my lawyer yesterday about some business matters. I didn't understand half of the advice he gave me because he used so much legal **mumbo jumbo**. I think I need to study law!

Sofia: I heard a little kid on the bus this morning. He was talking about a flying carrot wearing pyjamas*. Very strange!

Theo: Yeah. A lot of what young kids say is just **mumbo jumbo**.

알쏭달쏭한 말.
어쩌고저쩌고
mumbo jumbo
Com/Inf

Nonsensical or confusing language.
This phrase is often used humorously to
criticise (criticize [AM]) special words/
expressions that the average person
would not understand.

매수자위험부담원칙,
신의성실의 원칙,
중재, 진술서,
범죄 행위,
원천부터, 사실상…

Legal
Mumbo
????Jumbo

법적인 어쩌고
저쩌고

어제 사업 문제로 변호사와 긴 회의를 했어요. 난 변호사가
법률 용어로 **주저리주저리** 떠들어서, 나한테 해준 조언을 반도
알아들을 수 없었어요. 전 법을 공부해야 할 것 같아요!

이렇게
말하자:

소피아: 나 오늘 버스에서 어떤 아이가 하는 말을 들었어. 그 애는
잠옷을 입고 날아다니는 당근에 대해 이야기하고 있는 거야.
정말 별나!

테오: 맞아, 대부분 어린애가 하는 말은 그냥 **알쏭달쏭해**.

' pajamas [AM]

085

Miss the boat

He missed the boat

I sent a job application to a company a few days ago. Sadly, I just missed the boat. They stopped accepting applications the day before they received mine. I was stupid not to check the deadline date.

IN A REAL CONVERSATION

Amelia: Did you invest some money in the stocks that I recommended a few months ago?

Terry: No, I've been so busy. Which stocks were they? Maybe I can take a look at them this week.

Amelia: Sorry, Terry. You **missed the boat**. I have already made a 500% profit on them so far, but they're not on sale anymore!

Terry: What? Nooooooooooo!

기회를 놓치다
miss the boat
Com/Inf

To miss an opportunity. This expression was first used when talking about arriving too late to travel on a boat.

He missed the boat

그는 배를 놓쳤다

나는 며칠 전에 한 회사에 입사 지원서를 냈습니다. 하지만 슬프게도, 난 **기회를 놓쳤어요**. 회사에서 내 지원서를 받기 하루 전날에 접수를 마감했어요. 내가 마감일을 확인하지 않은 건 어리석었어요.

이렇게
말하자:

아멜리아: 너 몇 달 전에 내가 추천한 주식에 돈 좀 투자했니?

테리: 아니, 너무 바빴어. 어느 주식이었지? 아마 이번 주에 살펴볼 수 있을 것 같아.

아멜리아: 안됐네, 테리. 넌 **기회를 놓쳤어**. 난 그걸로 지금까지 이미 500% 이익을 남겼는데, 그거 더 이상 판매되지 않아!

테리: 뭐? 안 돼!

086

Music to my ears

I have been really worried about my health recently, so I decided to go for a health checkup. When the doctor told me that I was in perfect health, it was music to my ears! I'm going to have a big, fat, juicy steak tonight to celebrate!

Salesperson 1: My biggest client placed an order* today. It's worth over 6 million pounds!

Salesperson 2: Wow! That's fantastic! You're going to make a lot of commission from that.

Salesperson 1: Yeah! It's the best thing I've heard in a long time! It was **music to my ears**.

듣기 좋은 소식, 반가운 소식
music to
one's ears
Com/Inf

Something that you are happy to hear

건강하십니다
그 말씀 제 귀에
음악 같네요!

전 요즘 제 건강이 너무 걱정돼서 건강 검진을 받기로 했죠.
의사가 저에게 더할 나위 없이 건강하다고 말했을 때, 그건
정말 반가운 소리였어요! 전 오늘 저녁에 축하하기 위해 크고
기름지고 육즙 많은 스테이크를 먹을 거예요!

이렇게
말하자:

판매원 1: 나의 가장 큰 고객이 오늘 주문을 넣었는데.
6백만 파운드어치가 넘어!
판매원 2: 와! 훌륭해! 그걸로 수수료를 많이 받겠네.
판매원 1: 응! 오랫동안 들어본 것 중 최고야!
정말 좋은 소식이었어.

' place an order 주문하다

My battery is dead

It's 3am and I'm camping alone in the countryside. There's a strange noise outside my tent. It sounds like a big animal! I can't call anyone for help because my battery is dead! What should I do?

Eddie: Hey Bella, can I borrow your phone, please? I need to call my wife.

Bella: Sure, no problem. What's wrong with your phone?

Eddie: I forgot to charge it last night, so now **my battery is dead**.

배터리가 나가다,
배터리가 다 되다
my battery is dead
Com/Inf

My battery has no more power.

배터리가
사망하셨습니다

지금은 새벽 3시이고 전 시골에서 혼자 캠핑하고 있어요. 텐트 밖에서 이상한 소리가 들려요. 큰 동물의 소리 같아요! **배터리가 다 돼서** 전 누구에게 도움을 청하지도 못해요! 어떡하죠?

이렇게
말하자:

에디:　이봐 벨라, 네 전화기 좀 빌려줄래? 아내한테 전화해야 하거든.
벨라:　그럼, 얼마든지. 전화기에 무슨 문제 있어?
에디:　어젯밤에 충전하는 걸 깜빡했지 뭐야, 그래서 지금 **배터리가 다 됐어.**

My heart was in my mouth

While I was driving to work today, my car brakes suddenly stopped working! My heart was in my mouth for a few seconds. Luckily, they started working again, so I managed to pull over* and called a mechanic.

Layla: I saw a really scary horror movie last night!

Dave: Oh, was it good?

Layla: It was excellent! Horror movies don't usually scare me, but when I watched this one, **my heart was in my mouth** several times!

088. MP3

무서워 혼나다,
기절초풍하다

**one's heart was
in one's mouth**
Com/Inf

To be extremely scared, excited, or
worried. This expression suggests that the
heart is beating so hard that it appears to
leap upward (and into your mouth).

극도로 무서워하거나 흥분하거나 걱정하다. 심장이 너무
힘차게 뛰어서 위쪽으로(그리고 입까지) 뛰어 오르는 것처럼 되는
다른 표현이다.

"무서워!"

심장이 입까지 나왔어

오늘 차를 몰고 출근하는데, 브레이크가 갑자기 작동을 멈추는
거예요! 전 몇 초 동안 **혼비백산했죠**. 다행히 다시 작동해서, 전
간신히 갓길로 빠져 정비사에게 전화했어요.

˙pull over 한 쪽 길로 빠지다, 차를 대다

이렇게
말하자:

라일라: 나 어젯밤에 정말 무서운 공포 영화를 봤어!
데이브: 오, 재미있었어?
라일라: 정말 굉장했어! 평소엔 공포 영화를 무서워하지 않지만,
이 영화를 볼 때는 몇 번이나 **무서워서 혼났어!**

My mind boggles

MY
MIND
BOGGLES

My mind boggles at how much young Koreans study. They go to school every day, and then they go to private institutes to study in the evening. After that, they go home and spend hours doing homework! I think students need a better balance of work and play.

· ·

IN A REAL
CONVERSATION

Grace:	Do you know Terry Watson? He went to the same high school as you.
Jeremy:	Yeah, that guy is a genius!
Grace:	Right! I heard that he can speak more than 20 languages fluently!
Jeremy:	**My mind boggles** at people who are that talented!

믿기지 않다
one's mind boggles
Com/Inf

Something is difficult to understand because it is so unusual, incredible, strange, or complicated.
작가가 굉장히 많고 믿기지 않고 이상하거나 복잡하기 때문에 이해하기 어렵다.

내 정신이
움찔움찔해

한국 청소년들이 얼마나 공부를 많이 하는지 **믿기지 않아요.**
그들은 매일 학교에 가고 매일 저녁에 공부하러 학원에 가죠.
그런 후에, 집에 가면 숙제를 하는 데 시간을 할애해요! 전
학생들이 공부와 놀이의 균형을 더 잘 맞출 필요가 있다고 봐요.

이렇게
말하자:

그레이스: 너 테리 왓슨 알아? 걔가 너랑 같은 고등학교에 다녔는데.
제레미: 응. 그 녀석 천재야!
그레이스: 맞아! 난 걔가 20개 넘는 언어를 유창하게 구사할 수 있다고
들었어!
제레미: 그렇게 재능 있는 사람들을 보면 **믿기지 않아!**

My girlfriend broke up with me a few weeks ago.
She said she didn't want to be in a relationship with*
anyone right now. My friend told me this morning
that my ex* has already got a new boyfriend.
That was **news to me**!

**IN A REAL
CONVERSATION**

Greg: Are you going to Gavin's party tonight?

Mia: Gavin's having a party? **News to me**.

Greg: Oh! I thought he'd invited you.

Mia: Actually, I don't think he likes me, so I don't
really expect to be invited.

처음 듣는 소리
news to someone
Com/Inf

This expression is used when you hear something that you did not previously know.
이 표현은 이전에 알지 못했던 것을 들었을 때 쓴다.

- 네 여자친구
  새 남자친구
  생겼던데
- 나한텐
  새 소식이야

여자친구와 저는 몇 주 전 헤어졌어요. 그녀는 지금 당장은 누구와도 사귀고 싶지 않다고 했어요. 오늘 아침 제 친구가 전 여자친구에게 벌써 새 남자친구가 생겼다고 말해줬어요. 전 **처음 듣는 소리**라고요!

*be in a relationship with ~와 사귀다
*ex 전 애인, 전남편, 전처

....

**이렇게
말하자:**

그렉: 너 오늘 저녁 개빈의 파티 갈 거야?
미아: 개빈이 파티 열어? **처음 듣는 소식**이야.
그렉: 오! 난 걔가 너 초대한 줄 알았지.
미아: 사실 걔가 날 좋아하지 않는 것 같아서, 초대받을 거라고 진짜 기대도 안 해.

193

My friend borrowed my fishing rod*, and it broke when he was using it. He felt really guilty. I told him it was **no biggie** because that rod was old and cheap. Actually, I'm quite happy he broke it because now I can buy a new one!

IN A REAL CONVERSATION		
	Louise:	I'm really sorry, Stan. I can't make it to* the football match this weekend. I forgot I'm driving my friend to the airport.
	Stan:	**No biggie**... I'll ask Billy if he wants to go.

벌일 아님
no biggie
Com/Inf

It's not a big problem.
큰일 아니다.

- 미안… 내가
  네 낚싯대를
  부러뜨렸어
- 큰일 아니야.
  오래된 데다가
  싼 거야

제 친구가 제 낚싯대를 빌려 갔는데 그 친구가 사용하다가
부러졌어요. 친구는 정말 죄책감을 느꼈어요. 전 그에게 낡고
싼 거니까 **별거 아니**라고 말했죠. 실은, 그 친구가 낚싯대를
망가뜨려서 정말 기뻐요. 이제 새것을 살 수 있으니까요!

* fishing pole [AM]

**이렇게
말하자:**

루이스: 정말 미안해, 스탠. 난 이번 주말에 축구 시합에 못 가.
　　　　친구를 공항까지 태워다 줘야 하는 걸 깜빡했어.
스탠: **별일 아니야**… 빌리한테 가고 싶은지 물어볼게.

* I can't make it to ~에 못 가다

092

No show

Working in a restaurant can be a lot of fun. Meeting new people and giving people good service is very rewarding. On the other hand, some things can be quite annoying; for example, **no shows**.

Staff member 1: Was the restaurant busy last night?

Staff member 2: Not really. Three bookings didn't show up.

Staff member 1: THREE **no shows**? Wow, I don't understand how people can be so inconsiderate*. It's so easy to just make a phone call to cancel!

예약 부도, 예약하고
나타나지 않는 사람
no show
Com/Inf

092. MP3

A person/people who don't attend an
appointment and fail to give notification
that they will not attend
불참하겠다는 통지를 하지 않고 약속에 참석하지 않는
사람/사람들

안 나타남

"데이브네 식당 예약"

식당에서 일하는 것은 여러 재미가 있습니다. 새로운 사람들을
만나고 사람들에게 좋은 서비스를 제공하는 것은 매우 보람
있어요. 반면에 어떤 건 아주 짜증 나요. 예를 들면 **노쇼**족들이죠.

**이렇게
말하자:**

직원 1: 지난밤에 식당이 바빴어요?

직원 2: 아뇨, 예약한 세 팀이 오지 않았어요.

직원 1: 세 팀이 **노쇼**였어요? 와, 전 정말 어떻게 사람들이 그렇게
배려가 없는지 이해가 안 돼요. 그냥 전화로 취소하는 건 진짜
쉽잖아요!

*inconsiderate 배려가 없는

093

No spring chicken

I played football with some friends this afternoon. The last time I played sports was 20 years ago. Now I am completely exhausted, and my body aches. I guess I'm **no spring chicken** anymore!

IN A REAL CONVERSATION

Husband:	Agghhh! Every time I bend over, I get a pain in my back.
Wife:	Well, you're **no spring chicken**! Maybe you shouldn't work so hard, and get some rest on the weekends.
Husband:	I don't want to work so hard. I just have a lot to do!

청춘이 아닌
no spring chicken
Com/Inf

No longer a young person
더 이상 젊은 사람이 아닌

He's no spring chicken

봄닭이
아니네

오늘 오후에 친구 몇 명과 축구를 했어요. 제가 마지막으로
운동을 한 것이 20년 전이었죠. 지금 전 완전히 지치고
온몸이 쑤셔요. 전 더 이상 **청춘이 아닌**가 보네요!

**이렇게
말하자:**

남편: 아약! 허리를 굽힐 때마다 허리가 아파.

아내: 음… 당신은 **젊은이가 아니라**고! 그렇게 힘들게 일하지 말고
주말에는 좀 쉬는 게 좋겠어.

남편: 나도 너무 힘들게 일하고 싶지 않아. 그냥 해야 할 게 너무나
많아!

094

No use crying over spilt milk

I just bought a brand new mobile phone yesterday, but this morning I accidentally dropped it off my balcony. The screen completely smashed when it hit the ground! Oh well, I guess I'll just have to buy a new one. There's **no use crying over spilt* milk**.

IN A REAL CONVERSATION

Claudia: The hair salon really messed my hair up* yesterday. I'm so angry!

Tony: Well, there's **no use crying over spilt milk**. Anyway, your hair will grow again.

Claudia: True, but I won't go back to that hair salon again!

094. MP3

엎질러진 물이다
no use crying over spilt milk
Com/Inf

There is no point in worrying about something that has already happened.
이미 일어난 것을 걱정해도 소용없다.

우유를 엎지르고 우는 건 소용없는 일이야

전 어제 막 신제품 핸드폰을 샀는데, 오늘 아침에 실수로 우리 집 발코니에서 그걸 떨어뜨렸어요. 땅바닥에 떨어졌을 때 액정이 완전히 박살이 났어요! 아 뭐, 그냥 새로 하나 사야죠. **엎질러진 물이니까요.**

* spilled [AM]

이렇게 말하자:

클라우디아: 어제 미용실에서 내 머리를 정말 엉망으로 만들어 놨어. 너무 화가 나!

토니: 음, **이미 엎질러진 물이야.** 어쨌든, 네 머리는 다시 자랄 거잖아.

클라우디아: 맞아, 하지만 난 다시는 그 미용실에 가지 않을 거야!

* mess something up ~을 엉망으로 만들다

I was in the park this afternoon when a stranger sat near me. He started talking to me about the weather. We chatted for 5 or 10 minutes and then he suddenly asked me how much money I make! I told him very directly that it was **none of his business**.

IN A REAL CONVERSATION

Alex: So, Zoe, who did you vote for in the last general election?

Zoe: Sorry, Alex. That's **none of your business**!

Alex: Hmmm. I guess you voted for the corrupt candidate, and that's why you don't want to tell me.

상관할 일이 아니다,
신경 꺼라
none of one's business
Com/Inf

095. MP3

This expression is used when you tell someone that you don't want to share private information that is (rudely) being asked for.

누군가의 (무례한) 질문에 사적인 정보를 공유하고 싶지 않다고 말할 때 쓴다.

- 얼마 벌어요?
- 당신 일이
  아니잖아요!

오후 공원에 있었을 때 낯선 사람이 제 옆에 앉아 있었어요. 그는 저에게 날씨에 대해 이야기하기 시작했어요. 우리는 5분 아니면 10분 동안 대화를 나눴는데, 갑자기 나한테 얼마를 버는지 묻는 거예요! 전 그 남자한테 대놓고 **당신이 상관할 바가 아니**라고 말했어요.

**이렇게
말하자:**

알렉스: 그래서 조이, 넌 지난 총선에서 누구 뽑았어?

조이: 미안, 알렉스. **신경 꺼셔!**

알렉스: 흠. 부패한 후보한테 투표해서 나한테 말하기 싫어하는 것
         같군.

096

Not my type

My friend set me up on* a blind date at the weekend. The guy was very friendly and very handsome. Unfortunately, though, we didn't really have much in common*. He just was**n't my type**.

Trisha: Have you seen the new guy in our office? He is SO good looking! His hair is always perfect, and he dresses really well!

June: I agree that he is very handsome but I prefer guys who dress more casually. He's just **not my type**.

취향이 아닌
not one's type
Com/Inf

096. MP3

This expression is used to describe someone that you would not usually be attracted to.
평소에 매력을 느끼지 못하는 사람을 묘사할 때 사용한다.

그는 내
스타일이
아니야

제 친구가 주말에 소개팅을 주선했었어요. 그 남자는 매우 친절하고 잘 생겼어요. 하지만 불행하게도, 우리는 별로 공통점이 없었어요. 그는 그냥 **제 취향이 아니었어요.**

*set someone up on ~에게 소개팅을 해주다
*have ~ in common ~을 공통으로 가지고 있다, ~한 공통점이 있다

**이렇게
말하자:**

트리샤: 우리 사무실에 새로 온 남자 봤어? 그 사람 정말 잘 생겼어!
　　　　머리는 항상 단정하고 옷도 진짜 잘 입어!

준: 　　 그 사람 정말 잘생긴 건 동의하지만, 난 더 캐주얼하게 입는
　　　　남자들이 좋아, 그 사람은 **내 취향은 아니야.**

097

On the ball

Teaching English is a lot of fun, but it can also be challenging. When I teach high-level students, I have to really be **on the ball** because they sometimes ask difficult grammar questions.

Bella: Wow, I just looked at your schedule. You are SO busy! How do you manage to organise* such a heavy workload*?

Dave: I have a really good piece of software on my PC which helps me to stay **on the ball**.

사정을 훤히 꿰고 있는,
빈틈없는
on the ball
Com/Inf

Alert, competent, and quick to take action

민첩하고, 유능하고, 신속하게 대처하는 (이 표현은 스포츠에서 선수들이 공의 움직임에 반응하기 위해 정신을 바짝 차려 공에 집중하는 데에서 유래했다고 한다)

저 남자는
공 위에 있어

영어를 가르치는 것은 매우 재미있지만, 도전일 수 있죠. 제가 수준 높은 학생들을 가르칠 때, 그들이 가끔 어려운 문법 문제를 질문하기 때문에, 전 정말 **빈틈없이** 대처해야 해요.

이렇게
말하자:

벨라: 와, 방금 네 스케줄을 봤거든. 너 정말 바쁘구나! 어떻게 그렇게 많은 업무를 체계적으로 관리할 수 있는 거야?

데이브: 난 컴퓨터에 좋은 소프트웨어가 있어서 내 일을 계속해서 **빈틈없도록** 도와주고 있어.

* organize [AM]
* workload 업무량, 작업량

207

098

On the same wavelength

They are
on the same wavelength

My business partner and I work very well together. We have weekly meetings to discuss business, and we always agree on every decision we have to make. We are very lucky to be **on the same wavelength***.

IN A REAL CONVERSATION

Allison: I heard that you've broken up with your girlfriend.

Dylan: Yeah. We had different opinions on a lot of things. We just weren't **on the same wavelength**.

Allison: Oh, that's a shame. I thought you made a really nice couple.

마음이 잘 통하는
on the same wavelength
Com/Inf

This expression is used to describe two or more people who understand each other well and usually agree with each other.

두 명이나 그 이상의 사람들이 서로를 잘 이해하고 대체로 서로 동의하는 상황을 나타낼 때 쓴다.

They are
on the same wavelength

그들은 같은 주파수 위에 있어

제 동업자와 저는 함께 일을 정말 잘합니다. 우리는 매주 회의를 열어 사업을 의논하고, 우리가 내려야 하는 모든 결정에 의견이 일치합니다. 우리가 **마음이 잘 통하는** 것은 정말 행운이죠.

* wavelength 파장, 주파수

이렇게
말하자:

앨리슨: 너 여자친구와 헤어졌다고 들었는데.

딜런: 맞아. 우리는 많은 것들에 의견이 달랐어. 우리는 그냥 서로 **마음이 맞지** 않았어.

앨리슨: 오, 저런. 난 너희가 정말 멋진 커플이라고 생각했거든.

On top of that

Living in another country can sometimes be hard, but there are also a lot of good points. I have lived in Korea for a long time. I love my job, and I live in a nice neighbourhood*. **On top of that,** I LOVE Korean food! Especially Korean barbecue!

**IN A REAL
CONVERSATION**

Employer 1: Are you going to hire the candidate you interviewed this morning?

Employer 2: Definitely not. He arrived late for the interview and his work experience is very limited. **On top of that**, he answered the phone to chat with his friend during the interview!

게다가
on top of that
Com/Inf

Also. Additionally
또한. 추가로

- 한국에서 생활은 어때?
- 최고야! 일도 좋고
  사는 데도 좋고, 제일
  꼭대기는, 한국 음식이
  너무 좋아!

다른 나라에서 사는 것은 때로는 힘들 수 있지만, 좋은 점도
많아요. 전 한국에서 오랫동안 살고 있습니다. 저는 제 일을
사랑하고 좋은 동네에 살고 있습니다. **게다가** 전 한국 음식을
사랑해요! 특히 삼겹살이요!

* neighborhood [AM]

이렇게
말하자:

직원 1: 오늘 아침 당신이 면접 본 후보를 채용할 거예요?

직원 2: 절대 아니에요. 그 사람은 면접에 늦게 도착했고 경력은 너무
한정적이에요. **거기다가** 그 사람은 면접 중에 친구 전화를
받고 수다를 떨었어요!

I've had **one of those days**. First, I woke up late,
so I missed the bus. I had to take a taxi to work, but
I still arrived late. Then I spilled coffee on my shirt
AND my computer got a virus! I wish I hadn't* got
out of bed this morning!

IN A REAL CONVERSATION

Office boss: So, have you been busy today?

Employee: Yes, boss, but it's been **one of those
days**.

Office boss: Why?

Employee: I've been calling clients ALL DAY, but
they're not answering their phones!

100. MP3

재수(운)가 없는 날
one of those days
Com/Inf

A bad day with lots of problems
문제가 많은 날

오늘은
그런 날 중
하루였어

오늘은 **운이 없는 날**이었어요. 우선 늦잠을 잤고, 그래서
버스를 놓쳤죠. 전 택시를 타고 회사에 가야 했는데, 그런데도
지각했어요. 그다음 전 셔츠에 커피를 쏟았고 제 컴퓨터는
바이러스에 걸렸지 뭐예요! 전 오늘 아침 침대에서 일어나지
않는 게 나았어요!

* I wish I hadn't ~하지 않았다면 좋았을 텐데(과거 사실에 대한 아쉬움)

이렇게
말하자:

대표: 그래서, 오늘 바빴어요?
직원: 네, 대표님, 하지만 **운이 없는 날**이었어요.
대표: 왜죠?
직원: 하루 종일 의뢰인들에게 전화하고 있는데, 전화를
　　　받질 않네요!

I asked my friend to help me move some furniture to my new flat*. At first, he said "Yes". Then he realised* that I was moving to the 9th floor, and that the lift* was **out of order**. He quickly changed his mind!

- -

IN A REAL CONVERSATION

Alice:	Everyone has become really dependent on technology. This morning, my boss asked me to photocopy 100 really important documents, but when I got to the photocopier, it was **out of order**!
Jerry:	Oh no! What did you do?
Alice:	I had to take them to the stationery shop to have them copied.

101. MP3
Com/Inf

고장 난
out of order

This expression is usually used to describe machinery that is broken or not working properly.

보통 기계가 고장 났거나 작동이 제대로 안 되는 것을 나타낼 때 사용한다.

엘리베이터가
고장이야!

친구에게 새 아파트로 가구를 옮기는 것을 부탁했어요. 처음에는 그 친구가 "알겠어"라고 했어요. 그런데 제가 9층으로 이사를 할 거고 엘리베이터가 **고장 났다**는 것을 알게 되었어요. 걔는 재빨리 마음을 바꿨어요!

* apartment [AM]
* realized [AM]
* elevator [AM]

이렇게
말하자:

앨리스: 모든 사람이 기술에 많이 의존하고 있어. 오늘 아침, 상사가 나한테 정말 중요한 업무 서류를 100장 복사해달라고 부탁했는데, 내가 복사하러 갔을 때, 복사기는 **고장 나** 있었어.

제리: 저런! 어떻게 했어?

앨리스: 그걸 복사하려고 문구점으로 가져가야 했지.

I met my friend Tosh down by the river today.
He had been fishing and had a big net full of really
smelly fish. He asked if he could put them in my car
and drive him to his house. I told him it was **out of
the question**. I hate the smell of fish, and I've just
had my car cleaned!

Employee:	Boss, can I have tonight off? I want to go to a night club with my friends.
Boss:	What? It's Saturday night! You know it's the busiest night of the week! Having the night off is **out of the question**.

불가능한
out of the question
Com/Inf

Definitely not possible or not permitted

- 내 물고기 네
  차에 넣어도 돼?
- 말 같지도
  않은 소리!

전 오늘 강가에서 제 친구 토쉬를 만났어요. 그 친구는 낚시를
하고 있었고 큰 그물에는 냄새가 정말 지독한 물고기가
가득했어요. 토쉬는 그걸 제 차에 싣고 집까지 태워줄 수 있는지
물었어요. 전 **말 같지도 않은 소리**라고 했죠. 전 생선 냄새가
너무 싫고, 방금 세차했거든요!

**이렇게
말하자:**

직원: 사장님, 저 오늘 저녁에 쉬어도 될까요? 친구들이랑 나이트
클럽에 갔으면 해서요.

사장: 뭐요? 토요일 저녁이에요! 당신도 주중 가장 바쁜 저녁인 걸
알잖아요! 저녁에 쉬는 것은 **불가능**합니다.

They've got me
Over a barrel

My friends have asked me to go drinking with them tonight. I really don't want to go, but my friends said that if I don't go, they won't come to my birthday party next week. I guess I'll have to go out tonight. They've got me **over a barrel**.

Greg: Are you coming on the whitewater rafting trip this weekend?

Annie: No. The boss asked me to work this weekend. She knows that I'm hoping to be promoted next month, so if I don't do the overtime she might not promote me.

Greg: That's a shame. She's really got you **over a barrel**!

궁지에 몰린
over a barrel
Com/Inf

103. MP3

In a helpless situation, particularly when
someone has control over you.

나를
통 위에
잡아 뒀어

제 친구들이 오늘 밤 함께 술 마시러 갈 건지 물어봤어요.
저는 정말 가고 싶지 않지만, 만약 제가 가지 않으면 다음 주
제 생일 파티에 오지 않겠대요. 전 오늘 밤에 나가야 할 것
같아요. 친구들은 저를 **궁지에 몰아**넣었어요.

이렇게
말하자:

그렉: 이번 주에 나랑 급류 래프팅하러 갈 거야?

애니: 아니. 사장이 주말에 일해달라고 부탁했어. 사장은 내가 다음
달에 승진을 바라고 있다는 것을 알기 때문에. 만일 내가 초과
근무하지 않으면 나를 승진시키지 않을지도 몰라.

그렉: 거참 안됐네. 그 사람은 정말 널 **궁지에 몰아**넣었구나!

Par for the course

It is very cold in winter. It's also really difficult to walk when there is a lot of snow and ice. That's just par for the course in winter. That's why I rarely go out. As a result, I always gain weight in winter.

....

IN A REAL
CONVERSATION

Employee 1:	Do you think we will get a pay increase this year?
Employee 2:	No. We got a pay increase last year. We never get pay raises in 2 consecutive* years.
Employee 1:	Really? That's disappointing!
Employee 2:	Yeah, but it's **par for the course** in this company.

당연한
par for the course
Com/Inf

Normal or as expected in any given
situation

이 코스의
기준타만큼
나왔네

Par for the course

겨울에는 정말 추워요. 눈과 얼음이 많을 때는 걷기도 정말
힘들죠. 겨울엔 **당연한** 거예요. 그래서 저는 밖에 거의 나가지
않아요. 그 결과, 전 겨울에는 항상 몸무게가 늘죠.

이렇게
말하자:

직원 1: 넌 올해 우리 임금이 인상될 것 같아?
직원 2: 아니, 작년에 인상됐잖아. 2년 연달아 임금이 인상된 적은
없어.
직원 1: 정말? 실망이네!
직원 2: 응, 하지만 이 회사에선 **당연한** 일이야.

˚ consecutive 연이은, 계속되는

Can I pick your brain?

Sure!

I'm not very good with* computers, but I'm very lucky that my good friend Tom is a computer expert. Whenever I have a PC problem, he's happy for me to **pick his brains**. I always buy him a couple of beers to thank him.

· ·

IN A REAL CONVERSATION

Alex: I'm thinking about buying a new car, but I don't know much about them. It's really difficult to choose.

Anna: You should **pick Pete's brain** about it. He knows everything about cars! Just tell him your budget and basic requirements.

105. MP3

물어보다, 조언을 구하다
pick one's brain(s)
Com/Inf

To ask someone for advice about a subject the person knows well

그 주제에 대해 잘 아는 사람에게 조언을 구하다

네 뇌를
집어가도 될까?
물론이지!

전 컴퓨터를 잘 다루진 못하지만, 다행히 제 친한 친구 톰이
컴퓨터 전문가예요. 제 컴퓨터에 문제가 생길 때마다 걔는 제가
물어보는 것을 좋아합니다. 걔한테 고마워서 제가 늘 맥주 몇 잔
사거든요.

* be good with ~에 밝다, ~에 재주가 있다

이렇게
말하자:

알렉스: 난 새 차를 살까 생각 중인데, 차에 대해 잘 모르겠어.
고르기가 정말 어려워.

애나: 피트한테 **물어보면** 돼. 걔는 차에 대해서 다 알아! 그냥 예산과
기본 요구사항만 말해주면 돼.

My friend, Johnny, wants to be a professional MMA fighter. It seems like a pie in the sky idea to me. He's almost 45 years old and he has no experience in martial arts. Still, it's good to have dreams to aim for.

Johnny: The new president has plans to make big improvements to the country.

Sharon: Yes, but most of them seem **pie in the sky**. For example, she wants to give all high school leavers free university education.

Johnny: Yeah, I guess you're right. I don't think that will ever happen.

106. MP3

그림의 떡, 헛된 희망
pie in the sky
Com/Inf

Something that you hope will happen
but it is impossible or extremely unlikely

하늘에 파이

제 친구 조니는 프로 MMA 파이터가 되길 원해요. 그건 저에겐 **헛된 희망**처럼 보여요. 조니는 45살이 다 됐고 무술 경험도 없거든요. 그래도 꿈을 꾼다는 것은 좋은 거죠.

이렇게
말하자:

조니: 새 대통령은 나라를 크게 개선할 계획을 하고 있어.

샤론: 응, 하지만 대부분은 **그림의 떡**처럼 보여. 예를 들면, 모든 고등학교 졸업생에게 무상 대학 교육을 해주고 싶어 하잖아.

조니: 응, 네가 맞는 것 같아. 그런 일은 절대 일어나지 않을 것 같거든.

Pigs might fly

My friend, Wendy, is a very heavy smoker. She has tried to quit many times, but she always fails. She told me last night that she is going to quit today. And pigs might fly!

Carl: I think I'm going to win the lottery this weekend.

Wendy: Kent, you say that to me every week.

Carl: I know, but I'm feeling really lucky. I really think it's going to happen this time!

Wendy: Yeah, and **pigs might fly**!

107. MP3

해가 서쪽에서 뜨겠네
pigs might fly
Com/Inf

This expression is used to say that something is impossible or extremely unlikely to happen.

난 락스타가
될 거야

그러면 돼지도 날겠네!

제 친구 웬디는 완전 골초예요. 여러 번 끊으려고 노력했지만, 항상 실패하죠. 걔가 어젯밤 저한테 오늘은 끊을 거라고 말했어요. 그러면 **해가 서쪽에서 뜰** 거예요.

칼: 난 이번 주말에 복권에 당첨될 것 같아.

웬디: 칼, 너는 매주 나한테 그렇게 말하잖아.

칼: 알아, 그런데 정말 운이 좋은 느낌이야. 이번에는 정말 그 일이 일어날 것 같아.

웬디: 그래, 그러면 **해가 서쪽에서 뜨겠네**.

Yesterday, my British friend asked me what kimchi is. I couldn't think of a good way to describe it, but now it's just popped into my head! It's 'spicy fermented* cabbage'!

IN A REAL CONVERSATION

Kent: Something just **popped into my head**. You used to be a tennis coach, right?

Janet: Yes, that's right. Why?

Kent: Could you teach me how to play?

Janet: Sure, but only if you set up a blind date for me with your friend Tommy.

108. MP3

갑자기 머릿속에 떠올랐다
**popped into
one's head**
Brit/Inf

To suddenly have a thought/idea

"생각"
"뿅"

뭔가가 방금
내 머리에 떠올랐어!

어제 제 영국인 친구가 김치가 뭐냐고 물어봤어요. 김치를
묘사할 좋은 방식을 생각하지 못했는데, 지금 **순간 머리에
떠올랐어요.** 그건 '매운 발효된 배추'예요!

* ferment 발효되다, 발효시키다

이렇게
말하자:

켄트: 뭔가 방금 **내 머릿속에 떠올랐어.** 너 테니스 코치였지, 맞지?
자넷: 응, 맞아. 왜?
켄트: 어떻게 치는지 가르쳐 줄 수 있어?
자넷: 물론이지. 하지만 네 친구 토미와 소개팅을 주선해 주면
말이야.

Push my buttons

Don't push my buttons!

Something that really pushes my buttons is when people walking dogs don't pick up their dog's poop. When I walk my dog, I always pick up my dog's poop. It's not difficult.

Robbie: Richard is usually a really nice guy, but when he gets drunk, he really **pushes my buttons**.

Emma: Yeah, I heard that he gets very argumentative when he drinks too much.

열받게 하다
push one's buttons
Com/Inf

This expression is used when a person says or does something that irritates/annoys you.

내 버튼
누르지 마!

저를 진짜 **열받게 하는** 것은 사람들이 개랑 산책할 때 개의 배설물을 주워 담지 않는 거예요! 저는 개를 산책시킬 때, 늘 개똥을 줍습니다. 그건 어렵지 않아요.

이렇게
말하자:

로비: 리차드는 평소엔 괜찮은 녀석인데 취하면 정말 나를 **열받게 해**.

엠마: 응. 나도 걔가 술을 많이 마시면 시비를 잘 건다고 들었어.

In difficult times such as when a pandemic spreads, it's difficult to know what the outcome will be. We all need to do our best to stay healthy and prevent the virus from spreading further. It's not easy, but we need to **ride the storm** and hope for the best*.

IN A REAL CONVERSATION

Husband: It's been really hard to pay all our bills since you lost your job.

Wife: I know, but don't worry. I'll get another job soon. Let's just **ride the storm** until then.

Husband: Yeah, we'll be okay. And at least we are healthy and have a nice home.

110. MP3

난관에 맞서다.
위기를 극복하다
ride the storm
Com/Inf

To stay in control in a difficult situation and avoid being permanently affected by it
어려운 상황에서 평정을 유지하고 그 상황에 영구적으로 영향받는 것을 피하다

Ride the Storm

폭풍을 타다

전염병이 퍼지는 등 어려운 시기에는 어떤 결과가 나올지 알기는 어려워요. 우리 모두 건강을 유지하고 바이러스가 더 이상 퍼지지 않도록 최선을 다할 필요가 있습니다. 쉽지는 않지만, 우리는 **난관에 맞서**서 희망을 품어야 합니다.

*hope for the best 낙관하다, 희망을 잃지 않다

이렇게 말하자:

남편: 당신이 실직한 후로 요금을 모두 내기가 정말 어려워.
아내: 나도 알아. 하지만 걱정하지 마. 곧 다른 직업을 구할 거야. 그때까지 그냥 **맞서**보자.
남편: 응, 우린 괜찮을 거야. 그리고 최소한 우린 건강하고 좋은 집이 있잖아.

The boss ripped into him

I hate my boss! I'm thinking about quitting my job. I work really long hours and successfully complete all my work on time, but he still **rips into** me every day about minor things. It's like he has nothing better to do.

IN A REAL CONVERSATION

Laura: So, did your wife give you a hard time* for going home drunk last night?

Dave: Yeah. She was waiting for me at the front door and she really **ripped into** me!

심하게 비난하다
rip into
Com/Inf

To make a strong verbal attack on someone
누군가에게 강하게 언어적 공격을 가하다

The boss ripped into him

사장님이 그를 잡아 뜯었어요

전 제 상사가 싫어요! 일을 그만둘까 생각 중이죠. 전 정말 오랜 시간 일하고 제시간에 모든 일을 성공적으로 마무리하지만, 그 사람은 여전히 사소한 일로 매일 저를 **비난해요**. 그 사람은 더 나은 할 일이 없는 것 같아요.

이렇게
말하자:

로라: 그래. 어젯밤 술에 취해 집에 간 걸로 아내가 널 몰아세웠어?
데이브: 응. 현관에서 기다리고 있다가 나를 정말 **맹공격했어**!

*give someone a hard time ~을 힘들게 하다, ~을 꾸짖다

112

Rolling in it

He's rolling in it!

My neighbour* has a Ferrari and a Lamborghini.
His house has 8 bedrooms and a swimming pool.
He travels abroad about 12 times a year. He is SO
rich. He is absolutely **rolling in it**!

....

**IN A REAL
CONVERSATION**

Nicola: Are you going to Johnny's wedding
tomorrow?

Sammy: Yeah. I heard that he has hired a huge boat
with a live band to have the wedding on a river.

Nicola: Wow! That sounds really expensive!

Sammy: Yeah, but it's no problem for Johnny. His
parents are **rolling in it**!

| | 굉장히 부자인
rolling in it
Com/Inf | Very wealthy
매우 부유한 |

He's rolling in it!

그것 안에서
구르고 있다!

내 이웃은 페라리와 람보르기니를 가지고 있어요. 그의 집은
방이 여덟 개에 수영장이 있어요. 그 사람은 일 년에 열두
번쯤 해외여행을 가요. 그는 정말 부자예요. 틀림없이 **굉장한
갑부**예요!

*neighbor [AM]

**이렇게
말하자:**

니콜라: 너 내일 조니 결혼식에 갈 거야?
새미: 응. 걔가 강에서 결혼식을 하려고 라이브 밴드가 딸린 진짜 큰
보트를 빌렸다고 들었어.
니콜라: 왜! 그거 진짜 돈이 많이 들 것 같은데!
새미: 응, 하지만 조니에겐 별것 아니야. 부모님이 **굉장한 부자**거든!

113

Roll up your sleeves

I asked my kids to take out the recycling rubbish* a few hours ago, but they still haven't done it. Oh well, I guess I'll just have to **roll up my sleeves** and do it myself.

IN A REAL CONVERSATION

Son: I've got 6 exams next week!

Mother: Well, you had better **roll up your sleeves** and start studying! You don't have much time.

Son: Don't worry, mum*. I started studying weeks ago.

113. MP3

소매를 걷어붙이다,
팔을 걷고 나서다, 착수하다
**roll up
one's sleeves**
Com/Inf

To prepare to carry out hard work
힘든 일을 하기 위해 준비하다

소매를
걷어붙여

전 애들한테 몇 시간 전에 재활용 쓰레기를 밖에 내놓으라고
부탁했지만, 아직도 안 하고 있어요. 아, 그냥 **소매를 걷어붙이고**
제가 직접 해야 할 것 같아요.

* garbage, trash [AM]

- -

**이렇게
말하자:**

아들: 저 다음 주에 시험이 6개 있어요!
엄마: 그래, 너는 **소매를 걷어붙이고** 공부를 시작하는 게 좋을 거야!
　　　 시간이 별로 없어.
아들: 걱정하지 마세요 엄마, 몇 주 전부터 공부 시작했다고요.

* mom [AM]

He ran rings around him

I'm very proud of my son. He entered the chess tournament in his high school, and he won first prize! He **ran rings around** all of his competitors! He only learned to play chess a year ago. Maybe he's a genius, just like me!

IN A REAL CONVERSATION		
	Vicky:	My daughter has been studying really hard to improve her computer skills.
	Ted:	Oh, good! Is she enjoying it?
	Vicky:	Yes, a lot. And her school computer class grade has really improved. She's **running rings around** her classmates!

휠씬 더 잘하다
**run rings
around someone**
Com/Inf

To do something much better than
another person/other people
다른 사람들)보다 어떤 일을 훨씬 더 잘하다
(비슷한 표현: run circles around)

그의 주위를
달리고 있어

나는 아들이 정말 자랑스러워요. 개가 학교에서 체스 대회에
참가했는데 1등을 했어요! 모든 경쟁자**보다 훨씬 잘했어요!**
체스를 배운 지 1년밖에 안 됐는데 말이죠. 아마 저를 닮아
천재인가 봐요!

**이렇게
말하자:**

비키: 제 딸은 컴퓨터 실력을 향상하려고 정말 열심히 공부해
       왔어요.

테드: 오, 멋지네요! 따님이 재밌어하나요?

비키: 네, 많이요. 그리고 딸의 학교 컴퓨터 성적이 정말 좋아졌어요.
       같은 반 친구들**보다 더 잘하고 있어요!**

During my university days, I really struggled for money. I lived alone and the rent was high. Luckily, my friend's father **saved my bacon** by giving me a highly paid part-time job in his restaurant.

IN A REAL CONVERSATION

Tommy: Alicia! I've missed the airport bus! I'm going to miss my flight!

Alicia: My car's parked around the corner. I'll give you a lift*. We'll be there in no time*!

Tommy: Really? Thanks, Alicia! You've **saved my bacon**!

위기를 모면하다
save one's bacon
Com/Inf

To save someone from failing or from a difficult situation

실패 또는 어려운 상황으로부터 누군가를 구하다

네가 내 베이컨을
구했어! 고마워!

대학 시절에 저는 돈을 벌기 위해 정말 고군분투했어요. 전 혼자 살았고 집세는 높았죠. 다행히 친구 아버지가 그분 식당에서 고액 아르바이트를 하게 해주셔서 **위기를 모면했어요.**

이렇게
말하자:

토미: 앨리샤! 나 방금 공항버스를 놓쳤어! 비행기를 놓치겠어!
앨리샤: 내 차가 저 모퉁이에 주차되어 있어. 내가 태워줄게.
곧 거기에 도착할 거야!
토미: 정말? 고마워, 앨리샤! 네 덕분에 **살았다!**

* ride [AM]
* in no time (아주) 곧(=very quickly, in a very short period of time)

243

Send him packing

I'm tired of salesmen coming to my house to try and sell things. It's happened five times this week. The last one came this morning. I got angry and told him to stop coming to my door. I **sent him packing**!

Johnny: I saw some teenagers looking very closely at your bike outside your house this morning.

Kerry: Yeah. I saw them too. I thought they were going to steal it, so I **sent them packing**!

즉시 내보내다, 쫓아내다
send one packing
Com/Inf

To make someone leave/go away immediately
누군가를 즉시 떠나게/가게 하다

"다시 오지 마!"

짐 싸서 내보냈다

전 물건을 팔려고 우리 집에 오는 외판원들에게 지쳤어요. 이번 주에 다섯 번이나 왔죠. 마지막은 오늘 아침이었어요. 전 화가 나서 그 사람한테 우리 집에 오지 말라고 했어요. 전 그 사람을 **바로 쫓아 보냈죠!**

이렇게 말하자:

조니: 나 오늘 아침에 너희 집 밖에서 십대들이 네 자전거를 아주 자세히 보고 있는 걸 봤어.

캐리: 응. 나도 걔네들을 봤어. 걔들이 훔쳐 갈지도 모른다는 생각이 들어서 걔들을 **바로 쫓아 보냈지!**

I went to a really cool house party last night.
Everyone was dancing, and the food was really
good. Sadly, I had to shoot off early because
I had to catch the last bus home. Maybe I'll have a
party at my house next time.

Sophie:	Hey, Felix. Could you give me a hand* to move these boxes into my garage?
Felix:	Sorry, Sophie, I have to **shoot off** right now to pick up my kids from school.
Sophie:	Ah, okay. I'll ask Bobby if he can help me.

급히 떠나다
shoot off
Brit/Inf

To depart/leave somewhere quickly or abruptly
어딘가로 급히 또는 갑자기 떠나다/출발하다

난 발사됐어

어젯밤에 정말 멋진 홈파티에 갔어요. 모두 춤추고 있었고, 음식도 정말 맛있었어요. 아쉽게도, 집으로 가는 막차를 타야 했기 때문에 전 **급히 떠나야**만 했어요. 다음엔 우리 집에서 파티를 할까 봐요.

이렇게
말하자:

소피: 있잖아, 펠릭스, 이 상자들을 내 차고로 옮기는 걸 도와줄 수 있어?

펠릭스: 미안 소피. 난 애들을 데리러 학교로 **당장 출발해야** 돼.

소피: 오, 알겠어. 바비가 도와줄 수 있는지 물어볼게.

*give someone a hand ~를 돕다

I shot myself in the foot

A police officer stopped a driver because he was driving too fast. The driver really **shot himself in the foot** when he told the police officer he had just left a bar. He was breathalysed* and then charged with* drink driving AND speeding.

Cindy: How was your interview for the teaching job yesterday?

Donnie: Well, it started off okay, but I messed it up.

Cindy: How? What did you say?

Donnie: I told them that I only wanted to teach for 1 or 2 years to make some money to go travelling.

Cindy: Oh, no! Are you stupid? You really **shot yourself in the foot**!

118. MP3

자기 발등을 찍다
shot oneself in the foot
Com/Inf

To unintentionally make a situation worse for yourself
본의 아니게 상황을 악화시키다

내가 내 발을 쐈어

과속하는 운전자를 경찰이 세웠어요. 운전자가 경찰에게
술집에서 막 나왔다고 말했을 때 **자기 발등을 찍었죠.** 그 사람은
음주 측정을 받은 다음 음주 운전 '그리고' 과속으로 기소됐어요.

⁺ breathalyzed [AM]
⁺ charge with ~의 죄로 기소하다

이렇게
말하자:

신디: 너 어제 교직 면접은 어땠어?
도니: 음. 시작은 좋았는데 내가 망쳤어.
신디: 어떻게? 뭐라고 했는데?
도니: 여행 갈 돈을 모으기 위해 일이 년 정도만 가르치고 싶다고
했어.
신디: 오. 이런! 너 멍청이야? 정말 네가 **네 발등을 찍었네!**

Smoke like a chimney

My cousin started smoking when he was 15 years old. He is 54 now, and he still smokes. Actually, he **smokes like a chimney**; at least 3 packs a day! I know it's difficult to quit, but I hope he at least cuts down.

IN A REAL CONVERSATION

Sunny: Wow! You are smoking a lot these days. How many packs a day do you usually smoke?

Christian: Ummm. About 2 packs a day. But if I go drinking, I smoke a lot more.

Sunny: Oh, my god, you **smoke like a chimney**! You really need to smoke less. Nicotine is really bad for you!

담배를 많이 피우다
**smoke
like a chimney**
Com/Inf

To smoke heavily. To smoke a lot of cigarettes
담배를 많이 피우다

굴뚝처럼
연기를 피우네

제 사촌은 15살 때 담배를 피우기 시작했어요. 그는 지금
54살이고, 여전히 담배를 피우죠. 사실 하루에 최소 세 갑이니,
담배를 진짜 많이 피우는 거죠. 끊는 게 어렵다는 건 알지만,
그저 줄이기라도 했으면 좋겠어요.

이렇게
말하자:

써니: 왜! 너 요즘 담배를 너무 많이 피우는구나. 보통 하루에
몇 갑이나 피워?

크리스티안: 음, 하루에 2갑 정도인데, 술 마시러 가면 훨씬 더 피우는
것 같아.

써니: 세상에. **담배를 정말 많이 피우는구나!** 정말 담배를 줄일
필요가 있네. 니코틴이 얼마나 해로운데!

I went to a department store to buy a hat yesterday. I've never bought a hat before. I wasn't sure which hat would **suit me**. Luckily, a member of staff helped me choose one. It was quite expensive, but I'm happy with it!

Hailey: Blythe, that's a really cool hat! It really **suits you**. You always wear really nice clothes. How do you choose them?

Blythe: To be honest, I always go shopping with my wife. She's a fashion designer, so she always picks clothes that suit me.

잘 어울리다
something suits someone
Com/Inf

Something looks good on someone.
뭔가가 누군가에게 잘 어울리다.

- 네 모자
  너한테 딱이야
- 고마워

Your hat Suits you

thank you

어제 모자를 사러 백화점에 갔어요. 전에는 모자를 사 본 적이 없어요. 어떤 모자가 **나한테 어울릴지** 잘 모르겠더군요. 다행히도 직원 한 명이 고르는 것을 도와줬어요. 꽤 비싸긴 했지만, 난 만족해요!

이렇게 말하자:

헤일리: 블라이스, 정말 멋진 모자네요! 정말 잘 어울려요. 당신은 항상 옷을 멋지게 입잖아요. 어떻게 고르는 거예요?

블라이스: 솔직히 말하면, 난 항상 아내와 쇼핑하러 가요. 아내는 패션 디자이너라서 항상 **나에게 어울리는** 옷을 골라주죠.

Staycation

Travelling overseas can be difficult to plan, and can be expensive. Having a **staycation** is much easier to plan, and much cheaper. Besides, there are lots of good places to visit within a couple of hours driving distance of my home.

Wife: What shall we do for our summer holiday*?

Husband: Well, money is a little bit tight at the moment. How do you feel about having a **staycation**, rather than going abroad?

Wife: Yes, that sounds fine! Maybe we could go camping.

Husband: That's an excellent idea! I love camping! There's a really nice lake a few hours drive from here. Let's go there!

| 집에서 즐기는 휴가 |
| **staycation** |
| Com/Inf |

121. MP3

A combination of the words 'stay' and 'vacation'. It means staying in one's home country rather than overseas. It can also mean staying at home and going on day trips locally.

stay와 vacation을 조합한 단어. 해외보다는 국내에서 휴가를 보내는 것을 뜻한다. 집에서 보내거나 지방으로 당일치기 여행을 가는 것을 의미하기도 한다.

야아~
집캉스다!

해외여행은 계획 짜기 어렵고 비용이 많이 들 수 있죠. **집에서 즐기는 휴가**는 훨씬 계획하기 쉽고 훨씬 싸게 먹혀요. 게다가 우리 집에서 차로 두어 시간 거리에 가볼 만한 좋은 장소가 많거든요.

이렇게 말하자:

아내: 여름휴가 때 우리 뭐 할까?

남편: 글쎄, 지금 돈이 조금 빠듯하니까 해외로 가는 거보단 **집에서 즐기기**로 하는 거 어떻게 생각해?

아내: 응. 그것 좋은 것 같은데! 어쩌면 캠핑을 갈 수도 있고.

남편: 멋진 생각이야! 난 캠핑이 정말 좋아! 여기서 차로 몇 시간 거리에 정말 괜찮은 호수가 있어. 거기로 가자!

* vacation [AM]

Having a full-time job and taking care of your family can be tiring and stressful. It's important to find time to relax. Whether it's staying at home and watching TV, or taking a trip to the countryside, don't forget to **stop and smell the roses**!

Sarah: I've just started a new part-time job working 7 nights at a convenience store.

Jasper: ANOTHER part-time job? You're in your final year of university. Don't you think you are doing too much?

Sarah: Nah. I can handle it.

Jasper: Money is good, but you really need to **stop and smell the roses** sometimes. You only live once!*

122. MP3

여유를 가지다
stop and smell the roses
Com/Inf

To relax or take time off from a busy schedule to enjoy life
삶을 즐기기 위해 휴식을 취하거나 바쁜 일정으로부터 벗어나 쉬는 시간을 갖다

멈춰서
장미 향기
맡는 것을 잊지 마

종일 근무하고 가족을 돌보는 것은 지치고 스트레스가 될 수 있습니다. 휴식 시간을 찾는 것은 중요해요. 집에 머물면서 TV를 보든지 또는 시골로 여행을 가든지, **멈춰서 여유를 가지는 것을** 잊지 마세요!

이렇게
말하자:

사라: 편의점에서 7일 동안 밤에 일하는 새 아르바이트를 막 시작했어.
제스퍼: 또 다른 아르바이트? 넌 대학 졸업반인데, 너무 많이 한다고 생각하지 않아?
사라: 아니, 난 감당할 수 있어.
제스퍼: 돈도 좋지만, 가끔은 **여유를 가질** 필요가 있어. 인생은 한 번뿐이야!

* You only live once(YOLO). 인생은 한 번이다

Korean students study very hard. Studying can be frustrating and exhausting. But someday in the future, you will realise* that your efforts were worthwhile. So, **stick in there**!

Husband: I've been trying to write a novel for 2 years. I feel like I'm never going to finish it.

Wife: You're a good writer! **Stick in there**. Your book could be a best seller.

Husband: It would be great to see my book in shops someday.

123. MP3

포기하지 않다, 버티다
stick in there
Com/Inf

To withstand difficulties and persevere
to the end of a difficult or unpleasant
situation/activity

어려움을 견디고 어렵거나 불쾌한 상황/행동이 끝날 때까
지 인내하다 (비슷한 표현: hang in there)

거기에 붙어 있어!

한국 학생들은 정말 열심히 공부해요. 공부는 좌절하거나 지치게
할 수 있죠. 하지만 언젠가는 당신의 노력이 가치가 있었다는
것을 알게 될 거예요. 그러니 **포기하지 마세요**!

* realize [AM]

**이렇게
말하자:**

남편: 난 2년 동안 소설을 쓰려고 노력했는데, 끝내지 못할 것 같아.
아내: 당신은 좋은 작가야! **버텨봐**. 당신 책이 베스트셀러가 될 수도
있어.
남편: 언젠가 서점에서 내 책을 본다면 정말 멋질 것 같아.

124

Spread yourself too thin

Spreading yourself too thin

My friend, Jerry, has an office job from 8am to 6pm. When he finishes work, he goes to a bar where he works as a bartender from 7pm to midnight. I don't know how he does it! It must be exhausting. I think he's **spreading himself too thin**.

Andrew:	I've just been chosen to be the basketball team captain at university!
Annie:	Really? Congratulations, but you are already the captain of three other sports teams. You are also in your final year of university. Don't you think you are **spreading yourself too thin**?
Andrew:	Nah. I can handle it!

	한꺼번에 너무 많은 일을 벌이다 **spread oneself too thin** Com/Inf	To take on too many things (for example, activities or responsibilities) at the same time 동시에 너무 많은 것(예를 들면, 활동 또는 책임)을 떠맡다 (항상의 표현에 따라 일, 벌 때마다 같은 것을 떠맡을 때 너무 많게 벌려 소화를 못 내는 상황을 나타낸다)

Spreading yourself too thin

너를 너무
얇게 펴는데

제 친구 제리는 오전 8시부터 오후 6시까지 사무직으로 일해요. 일을 마치면 술집에 가서 저녁 7시부터 자정까지 바텐더로 일하죠. 전 걔가 어떻게 그렇게 하는지 모르겠어요! 분명 무척 피곤할 거예요. 걔는 **동시에 너무 많은 일을 하는** 것 같아요.

이렇게
말하자:

앤드류: 나 방금 대학에서 농구팀 주장으로 뽑혔어!

애니: 정말? 축하해. 하지만 넌 이미 세 개의 다른 스포츠팀 주장이잖아. 게다가 졸업반이고. **한꺼번에 너무 많은 일을 벌인다**고 생각하지 않아?

앤드류: 아니, 난 감당할 수 있어.

125

Take your hat off to him

I have a good friend called John. He's a really nice guy. He doesn't make a lot of money, but every month he donates hundreds of pounds to charity. You've got to take your hat off to him. Not many people are that generous.

Danny: Did you know that Laura spends a lot of time looking for homeless animals? Then she posts photos of them on* the internet and tries to find new homes for them.

Lynne: Yeah, I heard about that. You've got to* **take your hat off to** her. She's really kind-hearted.

경의를 표하다

**take one's hat off
to someone**
Com/Inf

This expression is used to say that you admire someone for something that they have done.

이 표현은 누군가에게 그 사람이 한 일에 대해 경의를 표하는데 쓴다.

당신은 그 사람에게
모자를 벗어야 합니다

전 존이라는 좋은 친구가 있습니다. 정말 괜찮은 녀석이죠.
존은 돈을 많이 벌지 못하지만, 매달 수백 파운드를 자선단체에
기부해요. **그에게 경의를 표해야** 합니다. 그렇게 후한 사람은
많지 않거든요.

이렇게
말하자:

대니: 너 로라가 집 없는 동물들을 찾는 데 많은 시간을 쓰는 것을
알고 있었어? 찾은 다음 동물 사진을 인터넷에 올려서 새
가정을 찾아주려고 노력해.

린: 응, 나도 들었어. 로라**에게 경의를 표해야** 해. 그녀는 정말
마음씨가 고와.

* post ~ on ... ~을 …에 게시하다
* You've got to 당신은 ~해야 한다(=You have got to: have got to는 have to의 구어체 표현이다)

I don't agree with corporal* punishment of children. I think it can cause psychological damage. I think that simply **telling** them **off** or restricting their playtime are more appropriate forms of punishment. That's how I brought my kids up, and it has worked well.

Mother: Where's Peter?

Father: I told him he can't watch TV tonight and I sent him to his bedroom.

Mother: Why?

Father: His teacher called me today. He had to **tell** Peter **off** 3 times in class today because he was misbehaving. That's why I punished him.

야단치다	To verbally scold or reprimand someone
tell someone off	
Com/Inf	

아이를 야단치고 있어

전 아동 체벌에 동의하지 않아요. 전 그게 심리적 손상을 일으킬 수 있다고 생각해요. 전 단순히 **야단치거나** 노는 시간을 제한하는 것이 더 적절한 체벌이라고 생각해요. 저는 그렇게 제 아이들을 키웠는데, 결과가 좋았어요.

---

corporal 육체의, 신체의

....

어떻게 말하자:	엄마:	피터는 어디 있어?
	아빠:	걔한테 오늘 밤엔 TV를 볼 수 없다고 하고 방으로 보냈어.
	엄마:	왜?
	아빠:	오늘 선생님이 전화하셨어. 피터가 수업 시간에 버릇없이 굴어서 세 번이나 **꾸짖어야** 했다고 하시더군. 그래서 내가 벌을 줬어.

That's the way the cookie crumbles

That's the way the cookie crumbles

I was planning on driving to the coast today to relax on the beach, but I've just checked the weather forecast. It says that it's going to rain all day. Oh, well! I guess that's just the way the cookie crumbles. I'll just stay home and watch TV.

Sandra: I can't believe it! My favourite* restaurant has closed down! I have been going there every weekend for the last 4 years.

Grayson: That's a bummer*! But **that's** just **the way the cookie crumbles**. I guess you'll just have to find another restaurant. Why don't you try the new Korean restaurant that has just opened up?

인생 다 그렇지 뭐
that's the way the cookie crumbles
Com/Inf

This expression is used to show acceptance of a failure or disappointment.

That's the way the cookie crumbles

쿠키는
그런 식으로
바스러지기
마련이지

전 오늘 해변에서 쉬러 해안으로 운전할 계획이었지만, 방금
일기예보를 확인했어요. 오늘 하루 종일 비가 올 거라네요.
아, 이런! 전 **세상사가 다 그런 것** 같아요. 전 그냥 집에 있으면서
TV나 볼래요.

이렇게
말하자:

산드라: 믿을 수 없어! 내가 제일 좋아하는 식당이 문을 닫았어!
지난 4년 동안 주말마다 거기 다녔거든.

그레이슨: 그거참 안됐다! 하지만 **인생이 다 그런 거지**. 다른 식당을
찾아야 할 것 같아. 이제 막 개업한 한국 식당에 가 보는 건
어때?

---

* favorite [AM]
* bummer 아주 실망스러운 것(something disappointing: 상당히 비격식적인 표현이다)

The ball is in your court

The ball is in your court

Finding a job is difficult these days. New technology has reduced the need for manpower. When looking for a job, you are sometimes faced with the dilemma of remaining unemployed or taking a low-paid job. It's a difficult decision to make, but the ball is in your court.

Mikey: So, are you going to buy my motorbike?

Brenda: Well, I really want to, but it's a bit expensive. Do you think you could drop the price a little bit?

Mikey: Sorry, Brenda, I have already given you a big discount. And you know, I really don't even want to sell it. Take it or leave it*, **the ball is in your court**.

128. MP3

결정권은 너에게 있다
**the ball is
in one's court**
Com/Inf

It is up to you to make the next decision
or take the next action.

공이 네 코트
안에 있어

요즘 취업이 어려워요. 신기술은 인력의 필요성을 감소시켰죠.
일자리를 구할 때 당신은 때때로 실업자로 남을지 저임금
일자리를 가질지 딜레마에 직면하죠. 결정하기는 어렵지만,
당신에게 달려 있어요.

이렇게
말하자:

마이키: 그럼 너 내 오토바이 살 거야?
브렌다: 음, 난 정말 그러고 싶은데 좀 비싸. 가격을 조금 깎아줄 수
있어?
마이키: 미안해 브랜다, 난 이미 대폭 할인을 해줬어. 그리고 너도
알잖아, 난 심지어 그걸 별로 팔고 싶지도 않아. 싫으면 그만
둬. **결정은 너에게 달려 있어.**

'take it or leave it 해도 그만 안 해도 그만이다

The weather doesn't look good today. It's very cloudy. I'm pretty sure it's not going to rain, though, so I won't take my umbrella to work. If it rains, I'll just get wet.

Jack: Korea has a lot of really interesting food, but there are some unusual ones, too.

Diane: Yeah, like chicken's feet!

Jack: Actually, I really like chicken's feet. I don't like silkworm pupae, **though**!

그렇지만, 그래도
though
Com/Inf

'Though' is similar to 'However'. This is used at the end of a sentence when you are saying something that contrasts with something you have previously said.

Though은 However과 유사하다. 이전에 말한 것과 대조되는 것을 말할 때 문장 끝에 쓴다.

It's very Cloudy!

It's not going to rain though!

- 날이 정말 흐리네!
- 그렇지만 비가 올 것 같진 않아!

오늘은 날씨가 안 좋은 것 같네요. 너무 흐려요. **그래도** 비는 안 올 것 같으니까 출근하면서 우산을 챙겨 가지는 않을래요. 만약 비가 오면 그냥 맞으려고요.

이렇게
말하자:

잭: 한국에는 정말 재밌는 음식이 많이 있지만 특이한 것들도 있어.

다이앤: 응. 닭발 같은 거!

잭: 사실, 난 닭발은 정말 좋아해. **그렇지만** 번데기는 싫어!

The manager of my favourite football team is a really smart guy. He really knows how to pick the best players for the team. There are a lot of very talented players all over the world, but he has managed to* pick **the cream of the crop**!

IN A REAL CONVERSATION

Jinseon:	I have applied to more than 20 companies for jobs, but I haven't had any replies.
Jisong:	Me, too. The competition for jobs is really tough.
Jinseon:	Yeah, they are really picking **the cream of the crop**.
Jisong:	That's us! Why don't they pick us?

최고 중의 최고, 단연 최고
the cream
of the crop
Com/Inf

The very best of a particular group of
people or things

넌 농작물 중에 크림이야!

제가 가장 좋아하는 축구팀 감독은 정말 명석한 사람이에요.
그는 팀을 위해 최고의 선수를 어떻게 뽑아야 하는지 정말 잘
알고 있어요. 전 세계에 재능 있는 선수가 많지만, 그는 어떻게든
단연 최고를 뽑아내죠.

manage to 어떻게든 ~을 해내다

이렇게
말하자:

진선: 난 스무 군데 넘게 입사 지원을 했지만, 답변받지 못했어.
지성: 나도 그래. 일자리 경쟁이 정말 치열해.
진선: 응. 그들은 정말 **최고 중의 최고**를 뽑을 거야.
지성: 그게 바로 우리야! 우리를 왜 안 뽑지?

The icing on the cake

I have just moved into a new apartment. I love it. It's close to a nice big park, and there is a river nearby. But the icing on the cake is, there is a Korean barbecue restaurant nearby! Mmmmm! I love Korean barbecue!

IN A REAL
CONVERSATION

Husband:	The new job I applied for; I got it!
Wife:	Congratulations!
Husband:	And **the icing on the cake** is that they are going to give me a company car!
Wife:	Really? Excellent! Now we have two cars!

금상첨화
**the icing
on the cake**
Com/Inf

Something that makes a good thing or situation even better

케이크 위의 장식

전 막 새 아파트로 이사했어요. 정말 좋아요. 크고 멋진 공원이 가깝고, 근처에 강도 있죠. 하지만 **금상첨화**는, 근처에 삼겹살 식당이 있다는 거예요! 음~, 전 삼겹살 구이가 정말 좋아요!

이렇게
말하자:

남편: 내가 지원했던 그 새 일자리를 갖게 됐어!
아내: 축하해!
남편: 그리고 거기서 내게 회사 차를 준다는 것이 **금상첨화**지!
아내: 정말? 훌륭해! 이제 우리는 차가 두 대야!

I'm usually a very punctual person, but when I met my friend Jim for lunch today, I arrived a few minutes late. He complained about that, saying that I was always late. THAT is the pot calling the kettle black! Jim is ALWAYS late!

IN A REAL
CONVERSATION

Jackie: Nicholas, you really need to lose some weight. Your belly is getting big.

Nicholas: What? Wow! Now that's **the pot calling the kettle black**! You are much fatter than me!

132. MP3

사돈 남 말 한다, 똥 묻은
개가 겨 묻은 개 나무란다
**the pot calling
the kettle black**
Com/Inf

This expression is used when the person
you are talking to is saying something to
you that they themselves are guilty of.

"너
시꺼멓다"

주전자 보고 까맣다고 하는 냄비

전 평소 시간을 잘 지키는 사람이지만, 오늘 점심때 제 친구 짐을
만났을 때는 몇 분 늦게 도착했죠. 짐은 제가 항상 늦는다고
말하면서 불평하는 거예요. 그건 **똥 묻은 개가 겨 묻은 개
나무라는** 격이죠! 짐은 항상 늦거든요!

이렇게
말하자:

재키: 니콜라스, 너 정말 살을 좀 빼야 할 것 같아. 네 배가 점점
나오고 있어.

니콜라스: 뭐? 왜! 지금 **사돈 남 말 하시네**! 네가 나보다 훨씬 더
뚱뚱하거든!

He's the salt of the earth

My best friend Tom is a really nice guy. He's really friendly to everyone, and he's always prepared to help people in need. He does a lot of charity work, and he also sponsors orphans all over the world. He really is the salt of the earth.

Tony: Sandy is a wonderful person. She's always helping people.

Claire: Yeah. She's helped me many times.

Tony: Did you know that she volunteers for an organisation* that visits senior citizens in their homes?

Claire: Wow! I didn't know that. She really is **the salt of the earth**!

133. MP3

세상의 소금 같은 존재
the salt
of the earth
Com/Inf

A person or group of people who are
kind, honest and reliable

그는 세상의
소금이야

He's
the salt
of
the earth

제 절친 톰은 정말 좋은 녀석이에요. 그는 누구에게나 무척
친절하고 항상 어려움에 처한 사람을 도울 준비가 되어 있어요.
톰은 자선 활동을 많이 하고, 전 세계 고아들도 후원해요.
정말 **세상의 소금 같은 존재**예요.

이렇게
말하자:

토니: 샌디는 훌륭한 사람이야. 항상 사람들을 도와.
클레어: 맞아. 샌디는 나를 여러 번 도와줬어.
토니: 샌디가 노인들의 집에 방문하는 기관에서 자원봉사 하는 거
알았어?
클레어: 왜! 난 그건 몰랐어. 걔는 정말 **세상의 소금 같은 존재**구나!

organization [AM]

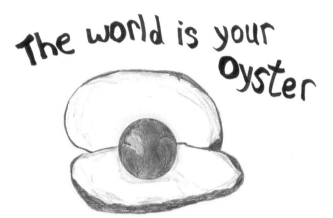

When you are young, you worry about lots of things, like study or getting a job. Teenagers in particular come under a lot of stress. My advice to teenagers is, "Do your best". You might not always succeed, but you are young and have your whole future ahead of you. The world is your oyster!

Rosie: Why the long face, Dermott?

Dermott: Well, I'm worried about getting a job.

Rosie: Really? But you have almost finished university, and you have really good grades. Your parents will support you until you start working. You have nothing to worry about. **The world is your oyster!**

세상이 모두 너의 것이다,
세상에 못 할 것이 없다
the world is one's oyster
Com/Inf

You are in a position to take the
opportunities that are / will be available
in your life.

The world is your oyster

세상이
너의 굴이야

젊을 때는 공부나 취업 같은 많은 것에 대해 걱정합니다. 특히
십대들이 스트레스를 많이 받죠. 십대들에게 하는 제 조언은
"최선을 다하라"라는 것입니다. 항상 성공하지는 못해도,
여러분은 젊고 당신의 앞날은 창창합니다. **세상에는 무한한
기회가 열려 있어요**!

이렇게
말하자:

로지: 왜 울상이야, 더모트?
더모트: 그게. 난 취업이 걱정돼.
로지: 정말? 하지만 넌 대학을 거의 마쳤고 성적도 아주 좋잖아.
네가 일을 시작할 때까지 부모님께서 널 지원해 주실 거고,
넌 걱정할 것 없어. **세상에 못 할 것은 없어**!

Everyone tightened their belts for the last couple of years because of the country's poor economy. Finally, the economy has improved and people can enjoy travelling and spending again.

IN A REAL CONVERSATION

Husband:	So, I think we can buy an apartment next year, but we are really going to have to **tighten our belts** until then.
Wife:	Okay. So, no more eating at restaurants. Starting from today, let's have lots of healthy home-cooking!

135. MP3

허리띠를 졸라매다
tighten one's belt
Com/Inf

To stop spending a lot of money. To live more frugally

우리는 허리띠를
졸라매야겠어!

국가 경제가 좋지 않아, 지난 몇 년간 모두가 **허리띠를 졸라맸었어요**. 마침내 경기가 좋아졌고, 사람들은 여행과 소비를 다시 즐길 수 있게 되었어요.

이렇게
말하자:

남편: 그러니까, 내년에 우리 아파트를 살 수 있을 것 같아요. 하지만 그때까지 **허리띠를 바짝 졸라매야** 해요.

아내: 알았어요. 더 이상 외식하지 말아요. 오늘부터 시작해서 건강한 집밥을 많이 해 먹어요.

Time will tell

I have just published a book! It's full of useful English expressions. I think it will be very popular with English learners, but I'll just have to wait and see. Only time will tell!

....

Cassandra:	So, what do you think of the new president?
Shaun:	I'm not sure. He seems to have a lot of good ideas, but I don't know if he will actually make them work.
Cassandra:	Yeah. I guess you're right. **Time will tell**.

시간이 지나면 알게 된다
time will tell
Com/Inf

Something will not be known until
sometime in the future.

시간만이
말해줄
거야

전 막 책을 출간했어요! 유용한 영어 표현으로 꽉 차 있죠.
전 이 책이 영어 공부하는 사람들에게 매우 인기 있을 것 같은데,
두고 봐야죠. **시간이 지나면 알게 되겠죠!**

이렇게
말하자:

카산드라: 그럼, 넌 새 대통령에 대해 어떻게 생각해?
선: 잘 모르겠어. 좋은 생각은 많이 있는 것 같지만, 실제로
그것들을 실행할지는 모르겠어.
카산드라: 응, 네가 맞는 것 같아. **두고 보면 알게 되겠지.**

My daughter won a competition on the internet. She won two free tickets for a BTS concert! She also won backstage passes, so she will meet BTS! She can't believe it. It seems too good to be true.

· ·

IN A REAL CONVERSATION

Alanis: I can't believe it! I've been offered a job on a beautiful island in the Pacific Ocean! The salary is fantastic, and I only have to work 3 days a week!

Simon: No way! That sounds **too good to be true**!

Alanis: Yeah, but I've checked the job contract and it all seems to be totally above board*!

너무 좋아서 믿기지 않는 **too good to be true** Com/Inf	So good that it is hard to believe 너무 좋아서 믿기 어려운

"BTS
대기실 출입증"

사실이라고 하기엔
지나치게 좋은데!

제 딸이 인터넷 경쟁에서 승리했어요. 그녀는 BTS 콘서트의
무료 입장권을 두 장이나 땄어요! 대기실 출입증도 받았으니까,
BTS를 만나게 될 거예요. 걔는 믿을 수 없어 해요. **너무 좋아서
믿기지 않나** 봐요.

는 above의 handwriting으로 "It seems Too good to be true!"

이렇게
말하자:

> 앨라니스: 믿기지 않아! 나 태평양에 있는 아름다운 섬의 일자리를
> 제의받았어! 급여가 기막히게 좋고, 주 3일만 일하면 돼!
> 사이먼: 설마! **안 믿길 정도로 좋은데!**
> 앨라니스: 응, 내가 입사 계약서를 확인해봤는데 모든 게 완전히
> 정상적인 것 같아!

above board 정당하고 정직하고 개방된(legitimate, honest, and open)

Two heads are better than one

When you work on social media; for example, blogging or creating videos, it can be difficult to make your content interesting and unique. I think that working with another person and sharing ideas is very beneficial to your results. After all, two heads are better than one.

Patrick: I have to stay home tonight and do my maths* homework. It's really difficult, so it's going to take a long time.

Miranda: Yeah, me too. I wish our teacher wouldn't give us such complicated problems to solve.

Patrick: Hey! **Two heads are better than one.** Why don't we do the homework together?

Miranda: That's an excellent idea.

백지장도 맞들면 낫다
two heads are better than one
Com/Inf

Two people working together have a much better chance of achieving a goal or solving a problem than just one person working alone.

한 사람보다 두 사람이 협력하여 목표를 이루거나 문제를 해결할 가능성이 훨씬 높다

두 사람 머리가
한 사람 머리보다 낫지

당신이 소셜 미디어에서 작업할 때, 예를 들면 블로그나 영상을 만들 때, 콘텐츠를 흥미롭고 특별하게 만드는 것이 어려울 수 있어요. 전 다른 사람과 일하고 아이디어를 공유하는 것이 결과물에 매우 유익하다고 생각해요. 결국, **백지장도 맞들면 나으니까요.**

이렇게
말하자:

패트릭: 난 오늘 밤 집에 있으면서 수학 숙제를 좀 해야 돼.
진짜 어려워서 시간이 오래 걸릴 것 같아.

미란다: 응, 나도 그래. 선생님께서 이렇게 풀기 복잡한 문제는 안 내시면 좋겠어.

패트릭: 야! **백지장도 맞들면 낫잖아.** 우리 같이 숙제할래?

미란다: 좋은 생각이야.

math [AM]

There are many ways to **unwind** after a busy day at work, or after a stressful event. Some people go to the gym. Other people have a few drinks, and some people like to meditate. How do you **unwind**?

IN A REAL CONVERSATION

Steve: I'm starting my first full time job tomorrow. I'm pretty stressed about it.

Sandy: Starting a new job is always stressful, but I'm sure you will be fine.

Steve: Well, I'll do my best.

Sandy: Of course, and just keep looking forward to the weekend. Then you can **unwind**.

긴장을 풀다
unwind
Com/Inf

139. MP3

To relax after a period of hard work or an intense situation
힘든 일 또는 극심한 상황 후 휴식을 취하다

You really need to **unwind**!

너 정말 감긴 것을 풀어야겠어!

직장에서 바쁜 하루를 보낸 뒤나 스트레스를 받는 사건 후에 **긴장을 푸는** 방법은 많습니다. 어떤 사람들은 체육관에 가죠. 어떤 이들은 술을 좀 마시고 어떤 이들은 명상하는 것을 좋아하죠. 당신은 어떻게 **긴장을 푸나요**?

이렇게 말하자:

스티브: 난 내일 첫 정규직 일을 시작해. 꽤 스트레스받고 있어.
샌디: 새로운 일을 시작하는 건 항상 스트레스를 주지만, 괜찮을 거라고 확신해.
스티브: 뭐, 최선을 다해야지.
샌디: 물론이지. 그리고 주말을 기다려 보는 거야. 그때 **긴장을 풀** 수 있겠지.

140

Up for (it)

There's a skydiving event in the countryside this weekend! I've always wanted to try skydiving. Several of my friends are **up for it** too! We are going to hire a minivan and go together. I'm really looking forward to it.

IN A REAL CONVERSATION

Rupert:	Are you **up for** a couple of drinks tonight?
Natalie:	Yeah! Good idea! I'm **up for it**. Where shall we go?
Rupert:	How about the new Irish pub?
Natalie:	Okay. I'll be there about 7pm!

하고 싶어 하는
up for something
Com/Inf

Ready and willing to take part in a
particular activity
특정 활동에 참여할 준비가 되어 있는

"스카이다이빙!"
"이번 주말!"

- 저거 하자!
- 좋아! 난 그거 할
  기분이 올라갔어!

이번 주말에 시골에서 스카이다이빙 행사가 있어요! 난 항상
스카이다이빙을 해보고 싶었죠. 끼고 **싶어 하는** 친구도 몇 명
있어요. 미니밴을 빌려서 함께 가려고 해요. 난 정말 그 행사를
고대하고 있어요.

**이렇게
말하자:**

루퍼트: 오늘 밤 맥주 몇 잔 할까?
나탈리: 응! 좋은 생각이야. 나도 **갈래**. 우리 어디로 갈까?
루퍼트: 새로 생긴 아일랜드 술집은 어때?
나탈리: 좋아. 난 저녁 7시에 거기에 가 있을게!

293

141

Used to it

My friend Kenny farts all the time. I know it's very natural to fart, but his farts are really loud and smelly. It's quite annoying, but he's been doing it for such a long time that I'm actually **used to it** now.

IN A REAL CONVERSATION

Kelly: I've noticed that your wife nags* you quite a lot. Doesn't it bother you?

Simon: Not really. I know she has the best intentions. And she's been doing it for so long* that I'm actually **used to it** now.

141. MP3

~에 익숙한
used to something
Com/Inf

familiar/normal to someone
익숙해지거나 평범해지는

- 앗… 미안
- 난 그거 익숙해

제 친구 케니는 항상 방귀를 뀌어요. 저도 방귀를 뀌는 건 매우 자연스러운 거라는 걸 알지만, 걔 방귀는 정말 시끄럽고 냄새가 지독해요. 꽤 짜증 나지만 걔가 하도 오랫동안 그렇게 해와서 사실 이제 **익숙해요.**

**이렇게
말하자:**

켈리: 난 네 아내가 너한테 잔소리를 꽤 많이 하는 걸 알아챘어. 안 괴로워?

사이몬: 별로. 그녀가 좋은 의도로 그렇게 한다는 걸 알거든. 게다가 하도 오랫동안 그래서. 난 사실 이제 **익숙해.**

* nag 잔소리하다, 들볶다
* for (so) long (꽤) 오랫동안

I'm Wracking my brain

?????

??.??

I met one of my old students on the street yesterday. I felt a little bit uncomfortable while I was talking to him because I couldn't remember his name. I've been **wracking* my brain** all day, but I just can't remember it. Ah! I've got it! It's Mr Kim!

IN A REAL CONVERSATION

Liam:	I've been trying hard to remember the name of the band that sang the song 'Wonderwall'. I just can't remember.
Suzanne:	That's easy. It was Oasis.
Liam:	Ah, right! Thank you. I've been **wracking my brain** all day about that!

| 머리를 쥐어짜다
wrack one's brain
Com/Inf | To think very hard about something
뭔가를 기억해 내려고 부적 애쓰다 |

전 제 뇌를
고문하고 있어요

어제 길에서 옛 제자 한 명을 만났어요. 대화하는 동안 그
친구 이름이 기억이 안 나서 좀 불편했어요. 하루 종일 **머리를
쥐어짰는**데도 기억이 안 나네요. 아! 알았어요. 김 씨예요!

* wrack 고문하다

이렇게 말하자:	리암:	난 Wonderwall을 부른 밴드 이름을 기억해 내려고 애쓰고 있는데, 기억이 안 나.
	수잔:	너무 쉬운데. 오아시스잖아.
	리암:	아, 맞다! 고마워. 하루 종일 기억해 내려고 **머리를 쥐어짜고** 있었거든!

My sister looked really sick this morning. I asked her **what was up with** her. She told me she had food poisoning. I think it must have been caused by the seafood she ate last night. I thought it didn't smell fresh!

IN A REAL CONVERSATION

Sandy: **What's up with** the weather? It was raining an hour ago, then it was snowing. Now the sun is shining!

Arnie: Dunno.* Maybe it's because of global warming.

Sandy: Yeah, that's a serious global issue. I hope we find a solution for it soon!

143. MP3

왜 그래?
What's up with ...?
Com/Inf

This expression is used when asking for
an explanation about something.
이 표현은 무언가에 대해 설명을 요구할 때 사용한다.

- 너한테 무슨 일
  생긴 거야?
- 식중독에
  걸린 것 같아

오늘 아침 제 여동생이 정말 아파 보였어요. 전 그 애한테 **무슨
일인지** 물어봤죠. 동생은 식중독에 걸렸다고 했어요. 어젯밤에
그 애가 먹은 해산물이 원인이라고 생각해요. 냄새가 신선하지
않다고 생각했거든요.

이렇게
말하자:

샌디: 날씨가 **왜 이래**? 한 시간 전에는 비가 오더니 그다음엔 눈이
       왔어. 그리고 지금은 해가 나는데!

아르니: 나도 모르겠어. 아마 지구 온난화 때문이겠지.

샌디: 응. 그건 세계적으로 심각한 문제야. 빨리 해결책을 찾았으면
       좋겠어!

* Dunno 나도 모르겠다(=I don't know: 비격식적 표현이다)

I was surprised when I first learned that people have to take their shoes off in a lot of Korean restaurants. It really felt strange, but I soon got used to it. After all, **when in Rome**!

Husband: Are you looking forward to our trip to India?

Wife: Yes. I'm reading about the culture now. Did you know that in India, you can eat just with your hands? No knives and forks!

Husband: Yeah. I heard about that. It seems a bit strange, but **when in Rome**.

144. MP3

로마에서는
로마법을 따르라
when in Rome
Com/Inf

When you are in another country/place, you should follow the customs of the people in that area.
다른 나라/장소에 있으면 그 지역의 관습을 따라야 한다.
(전체 표현은 When in Rome, do as the Romans do.)

"전통 한국식 바비큐"
- 신발을 벗으라고?
- 응… 로마에서는
  로마법을 따라야 돼!

전 많은 한국 식당에서 사람들이 신발을 벗어야 한다는 걸 알았을 때 깜짝 놀랐어요. 정말 이상하다고 느꼈는데, 금세 익숙해졌죠. 결국, **로마에서는 로마법을 따라야 해요**!

이렇게
말하자:

남편: 우리의 인도 여행 기대하고 있어?

아내: 응. 지금 인도 문화에 대해 읽고 있어. 인도에서는 손으로만 먹을 수 있다는 거 알고 있었어? 나이프랑 포크 없이!

남편: 응, 나도 들었어. 좀 이상한 것 같지만, **로마에 가면 로마법을 따라야지**.

When one door closes, another opens

Unfortunate things sometimes happen in life. Losing your job, or ending a relationship with someone. However, it's best to be positive. Bad times are always followed by good times. **When one door closes, another opens.**

IN A REAL
CONVERSATION

Layla: I'm SO depressed. I got fired last week. I don't know what I'm going to do now.

Tony: Be positive! **When one door closes, another opens.** Take a short holiday first. You are still young. Be excited about new opportunities that are coming your way!

Layla: I suppose you're right. I should try to look on the bright side*!

한쪽 문이 닫히면
다른 쪽 문이 열린다
When one door closes, another (door) opens
Com/Inf

Even when you lose an opportunity, another opportunity to do something else will come your way.
당신이 기회를 잃었을 때조차도 다른 걸 할 기회가 올 것이다.

한쪽 문이 닫히면,
다른 쪽 문이
열린다

살다 보면 불행한 일이 생길 때가 있습니다. 직업을 잃거나 누군가와의 관계가 끝나기도 해요. 하지만 긍정적으로 보는 것이 최선이죠. 나쁜 시기 다음에는 항상 좋은 시기가 뒤따라와요. **한쪽 문이 닫히면 다른 쪽 문이 열립니다.**

이렇게
말하자:

라일라: 정말 우울해. 나 지난주에 해고됐어. 이제 어떻게 해야 할지 모르겠어.

토니: 긍정적으로 생각해! **한쪽 문이 닫히면 다른 쪽 문이 열리는 법이야.** 먼저 짧게 휴가를 보내도록 해. 넌 아직 젊어. 네 앞에 다가올 새로운 기회를 기대해 봐.

라일라: 네가 옳은 것 같아. 난 긍정적인 면을 보도록 노력해야 해!

* look on the bright side 긍정적으로 보다, 낙관하다(=be positive/optimistic)

Why the long face?

I met my best friend yesterday. He looked really upset. I asked him, "Why the long face?" He told me that his girlfriend had broken up with him. I'm sure he'll get over it soon.

Student 1: Hey, Jodie. **Why the long face?**

Student 2: Because I was rejected by the university I wanted to go to.

Student 1: Oh, that's a bummer! But don't give up! Maybe you can try again next year!

왜 울상이야?
Why the long face?
Com/Inf

When you are sad/unhappy/ disappointed, your facial features (especially the mouth) 'droop' downwardly, making the face look 'long'.

슬프거나 불행하거나 실망스러울 때, 얼굴의 이목구비특 히 입가 아래로 처져서 얼굴이 길어 보인다.

왜 얼굴이
길어졌어?

전 어제 제 절친을 만났어요. 걔는 정말 속상해 보였어요. 저는 **"왜 울상이야?"** 라고 물었어요. 걘 여자친구와 헤어졌다고 말했죠. 전 걔가 곧 그 일을 극복할 거라고 확신해요.

이렇게
말하자:

학생 1: 야, 조디. **왜 울상이야?**

학생 2: 내가 가고 싶었던 대학을 떨어져서 그래.

학생 1: 아! 그것참 실망스럽겠다. 하지만 포기하지 마! 아마 내년에 다시 시도할 수 있을 거야!

A new deli has opened in my neighbourhood. Everyone is hearing about it through **word of mouth** from customers who have already been there. Everyone says that the food there is excellent. I think I'll go there now and check it out!

IN A REAL CONVERSATION

Sandy: So Danny, do you spend a lot of money on advertising your business?

Danny: Actually, no. I used to pay for advertising, but now most of my clients find my business blog on the internet, or they hear about it through **word of mouth**.

Sandy: Times have changed, largely because of SNS (social networking services).

입소문		Oral communication. Verbal sharing of information
word of mouth		구두 의사소통, 언어의 정보 공유
Com/Inf		

147. MP3

"입의 말"

잭이, 사라가, 톰이, 수잔이,
피터가, 재키가 말해줬어.

우리 동네에 새로운 식품점이 문을 열었어요. 모든 사람이
이미 다녀온 손님들의 **입소문**을 통해 그곳에 대해 듣고 있죠.
다들 그곳 음식이 맛있다고 해요. 제가 지금 거기 가서 확인해
볼까 봐요!

**이렇게
말하자:**

샌디: 그럼 대니, 너는 사업을 홍보하는 데 돈을 많이 쓰니?

대니: 사실, 안 그래. 예전엔 광고에 돈을 쓰곤 했지만, 지금은 고객
대부분이 인터넷에서 내 블로그를 찾거나 **입소문**으로 듣고
있지.

샌디: 시대가 변했고, 주로 SNS(사회관계망서비스) 때문이지.

I told my friend that I thought he was getting a bit tubby and that maybe he should go on a diet. He was quite angry and responded with, "You can talk, fatty!" I was quite shocked. I'm not fat, am I?

IN A REAL
CONVERSATION

Russel: You were REALLY drunk last night!

Petra: **You can talk**! It was me that* put you in a taxi at the end of the night because you could hardly walk.

Russel: Oh, um, really? I can't remember.

| 잘도 말하네, 사돈 남 말하네 **You can talk** Com/Inf | This expression is a response to someone who has just criticised something that they are personally guilty of. ~~이 표현은 ~ 개인적으로 잘못한 것을 막 비난하는~~ ~~사람에게 하는 반응이다. 반대로는~~ ~~말하면서 같이 화를 내면서 하는 표현이다.~~ |

148. MP3

넌 뚱뚱해
잘도 말하네!

저는 친구한테 말했죠. 걔가 점점 뚱뚱해지는 것 같아서 아마 다이어트를 해야 할 것 같다고요. 걔는 진짜 화를 내며 "**잘도 말하네**, 뚱땡이!"라고 대꾸했어요. 전 꽤나 충격받았죠. 전 뚱뚱하지 않아요! 안 그래요?

이렇게 말하자:

러셀: 너 어젯밤에 완전히 취했었어!

페트라: **사돈 남 말하시네!** 네가 거의 걷지도 못해서 밤늦게 너를 택시에 태웠던 사람이 바로 나야!

러셀: 오, 음, 정말? 난 기억이 안 나.

It is ~ that … …한 것은 바로 ~이다

You scratch my back, I'll scratch yours

I'm going a bit bald. Wigs are very expensive. Luckily, I have a Korean friend who has a wig business. He agreed to give me free wigs if I teach him English. Perfect! You know what they say, **you scratch my back, I'll scratch yours**!

Brenda: I really want to go and see the new Brad Pitt movie tonight, but I'm skint.*

Gavin: Well, I could lend you some money if you could do a small favour* for me.

Brenda: What kind of favour?

Gavin: Could I borrow your car tomorrow night?

Brenda: Sure! No problem! After all, you know what they say, **you scratch my back, I'll scratch yours!**.

149. MP3

상부상조하자
You scratch my back, I'll scratch yours
Com/Inf

If you do me a favour, I'll do you a favour.

그래서, 너 영어 공부하고 싶어?

내 등을 긁어주면 네 등도 긁어주마

전 머리가 좀 벗겨지고 있어요. 가발은 너무 비싸죠. 다행히 전 가발 사업을 하는 한국인 친구가 있어요. 제가 영어를 가르쳐주면 저한테 공짜로 가발을 주기로 합의 봤어요. 완벽해요! 이런 말이 있죠, **상부상조**라고!

· ·

이렇게 말하자:

브렌다: 오늘 밤에 브래드 피트가 나오는 새 영화를 정말 보러 가고 싶은데, 나 완전 빈털터리야.

게빈: 음, 내 작은 부탁을 들어주면 돈을 좀 빌려줄게.

브렌다: 무슨 부탁인데?

게빈: 내일 밤 네 차를 빌려줄 수 있어?

브렌다: 그럼! 문제없어! 어쨌든, 사람들이 이런 말을 하잖아, **상부상조 하는** 거라고.

---

* skint 돈이 없는, 가난한(=having no money, poor: 비격식적인 영국 영어)   * favor [AM]

Where is Scotland?

? You're Scottish.. you should know!

I have a good friend from Scotland. We were looking at a map of the world. He asked me where Scotland was on the map! "You should know!" I exclaimed, "You're Scottish!"

· ·

IN A REAL CONVERSATION

Nora: Rennie, How do you say 'potato' in Korean?

Rennie: **You should know**! You lived in Korea for almost 10 years! It's 사과. Oh, no, wait! Let me think.

Nora: Actually, **you should know**! You have a Korean wife!

150. MP3

넌 알아야지
You should know
Com/Inf

This expression is used when someone has just asked a question that you think they already know the answer to.

스코틀랜드는
어디에 있어?
너 스코틀랜드
사람이잖아…
넌 알아야지!

전 스코틀랜드에서 온 친한 친구가 있어요. 우리는 세계 지도를 보고 있었죠. 걔가 나한테 지도에서 스코틀랜드가 어디에 있는지 묻더군요! "**네가 알아야지!**" 전 소리쳤죠, "너 스코틀랜드 사람이잖아!"

이렇게
말하자:

노라: 레니, potato를 한국어로 뭐라고 해?
레니: **넌 알아야지!** 한국에 10년 가까이 살았잖아! '사과'야.
오, 아니, 잠깐만! 생각해 볼게.
노라: 사실, **네가 알아야지!** 네 아내가 한국인이잖아!

INDEX

INDEX 한국어 키워드 인덱스

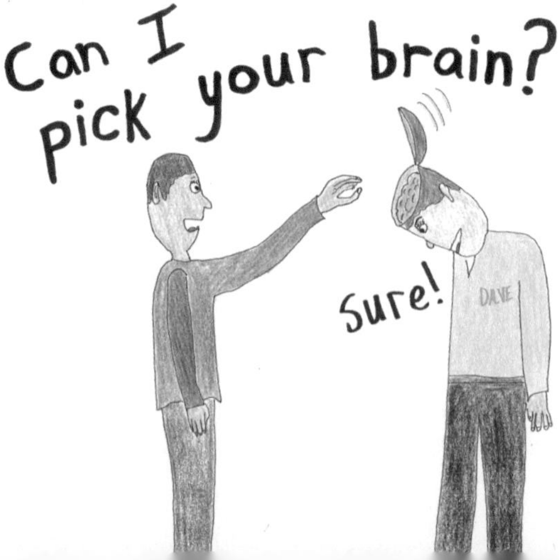
Can I pick your brain?
Sure!
DAVE